MOU... BIKE GUIDE

MID-WALES & THE MARCHES

BY JON DIXON

THE ERNEST PRESS

Published by The Ernest Press   1998

© Copyright Jon Dixon

ISBN 0 948153 50 4

British Library Cataloguing-in-Publication Data has been registered with the British Library in Wetherby and is available on request.

Printed by St Edmundsbury Press Ltd
Bury St Edmunds, Suffolk

Disclaimer:

Whilst we have made every effort to achieve accuracy in the production of material for use in this guide book, the author, publishers and copyright owners can take no responsibility for: trespass, irresponsible riding, any loss or damage to persons or property suffered as a result of the route descriptions or advice offered in this book.

The inclusion of a route in this guide does not guarantee that the path/track is or will remain a right of way. If conflict with landowners occurs, please be polite and leave by the shortest available route, then check the situation with the relevant authority.

It ought to go without saying really, but I'll say it anyway - Mountain biking is a potentially hazardous activity. The consequences of crashing, getting lost or over-exerting yourself, especially in remote areas or in bad weather, could range from mildly unpleasant to fatal! Always ride within the limits of your abilities.

Always give way to pedestrians and horse riders and warn them of your approach.

INTRODUCTION

Since Buying my first Mountain Bike nearly 9 years ago I must admit I've become pretty obsessed. But when I started writing this book I wondered if maybe I'd gone too far. I loved mountain biking because it was fun - no hassles, no pressure - I'd just get out there and ride. But I was worried that writing a book about it might turn it all into a horrible chore - I'd get so sick of my bike I'd end up trading it in for a nice comfy arm chair!

Well the good news is I've still got the bike. It's not surprising really. Mid-Wales and the Marches really are a mountain biker's paradise. While researching this book I've discovered some of the best trails I've ever ridden. I've cycled hundreds of miles through stunning scenery, slogged up massive hills, clambered around on craggy mountain tops, snaked along twisty narrow paths down picturesque valleys, splashed through huge fords, crossed bleak moorland with only a distant red kite for company, discovered ancient moss-covered ruins, pedalled along the bustling streets of little market towns, cruised along smooth tracks through forests and around dramatic lakes, swooped down heavenly descents that seemed to go on for ever and scared the ✳🐛☺‼ out of myself on horrendous rocky plummets.

And now I've put all the best bits down on paper so you can enjoy them too!

ACKNOWLEDGEMENTS

Big thank yous must go to all the people who helped to make this book happen, especially: Snowdonia National Park, Wrekin Council and the Rights of Way people at Gwynedd, Wrexham, Denbighshire, Shropshire, Hereford + Worcester, Ceredigion and Powys County Councils for checking routes; Forest Enterprise and Dŵr Cymru/Welsh Water for access to private tracks; Longmynd Mountain Bike Club, including Mark Higgins for route ideas and Brendan and Liz Meehan, Peter Cooke, Peter Beach, Paul Green, Liz Cowell, John Yandell, Julie Jordan and Tom Middleton for posing!; Susan Askvik for her eagle-eyed proofreading and Peter Hodgkiss of the Ernest Press for being brave enough to publish my collection of crazed scribblings! THANKS EVERYONE!

CONTENTS

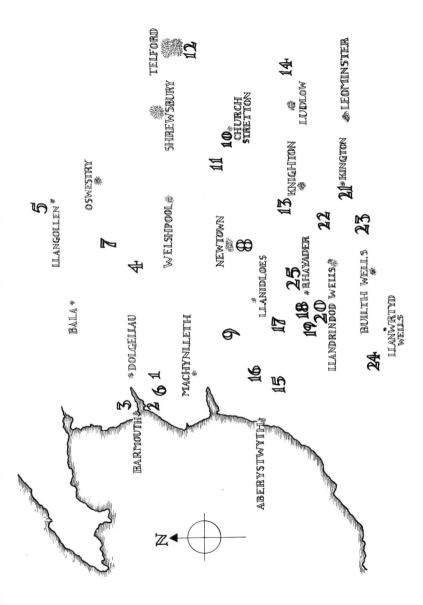

MAPS

THE MAPS IN THIS BOOK WERE ALL DRAWN FROM DETAILED SKETCHES AND NOTES MADE WHILST RIDING THE ROUTES. I'VE TRIED TO INCLUDE USEFUL LITTLE DETAILS THAT ARE NOT SHOWN ON OTHER MAPS. HOWEVER I WOULD STILL RECOMMEND THAT YOU USE THIS BOOK IN CONJUNCTION WITH APPROPRIATE ORDNANCE SURVEY MAPS AS THEY REALLY CAN'T BE BEATEN FOR THINGS LIKE ACCURATELY DEPICTING HILLS AND LAND SHAPES AND THEY ALSO SHOW ALL THE OPTIONS IF YOU WANT TO SHORTEN OR EXTEND A ROUTE. 1:50 000 SCALE LANDRANGERS GIVE A GOOD OVERALL IMPRESSION OF A LARGE AREA WHILE 1:25 000 SCALE PATHFINDER, EXPLORER AND OUTDOOR LEISURE MAPS GIVE MORE DETAILED INFORMATION - SUCH AS FIELD BOUNDARIES - WHICH IS USEFUL.

MAP TIPS
- MAKE SURE YOUR MAPS ARE UP TO DATE. (UNLESS YOU LIKE TRYING TO NAVIGATE THROUGH FORESTS OR AROUND RESERVOIRS THAT AREN'T SHOWN ON YOUR MAP!).
- GET YOUR MAPS LAMINATED - THAT WAY YOU WON'T HAVE TO BUY A NEW ONE AFTER EACH MUDDY RIDE.

MAP KEY

 BUILDINGS

 RAILWAY

 ROAD

 WIDE TRACK

 NARROW TRACK

NO TRACK!

 FENCE

 WALL

 HEDGE

 TREES

 RIVER

 LAKE

 HILLSIDE

 CRAGS

SCREE

NOTE THAT FENCES, HEDGES AND WALLS ARE NORMALLY ONLY SHOWN ALONG THE OFF ROAD SECTIONS OF ROUTES.

Rights of Way

The off-road routes in this book mostly use public rights of way. These are bridleways, roads used as public paths and byways open to all traffic (all marked on Ordnance Survey maps) and unclassified, unsurfaced roads (the O.S. are starting to show these as rights of way on new maps - but on most maps they're just shown as tracks and its hard to tell if they're public or private). There are also some sections using permissive tracks where you have no legal right to ride but are allowed access by the landowner (so treat them with respect). Remember - bikes are NOT allowed on footpaths. The status of routes, whether legal or permissive, can change - so beware. If you have any queries about routes - or problems such as blocked rights of way, contact the rights of way officer at the appropriate local authority.

Route Grades

Route grading is difficult as it tends to be extremely subjective. The following list is a rough guide only - for average riders in dry conditions. Most routes are likely to be a lot harder in bad weather - especially those that cross high hilltops. For a better idea of what to expect - read the route descriptions.

CORRIS	HARD
BARMOUTH COAST	HARD
PONT SCETHIN	HARD
LAKE VYRNWY	EASY
HORSESHOE PASS	HARD
CADAIR IDRIS	EXTREME
TANAT VALLEY & THE BERWYNS	HARD
KERRY HILL	HARD
FOEL FADIAN	HARD
THE LONGMYND	HARD
THE STIPERSTONES	HARD
IRONBRIDGE	EASY
BEACON HILL & OFFA'S DYKE	HARD
TITTERSTONE CLEE	MODERATE
DEVIL'S BRIDGE & THE VALE OF RHEIDOL	MODERATE
NANT-Y-MOCH RESERVOIR	MODERATE
LLANGURIG	MODERATE
ELAN HILLS	EXTREME
ELAN LAKES	EXTREME
CLAERWEN VALLEY	MODERATE
HERGEST RIDGE	EASY
RADNOR FOREST	HARD
GLASCWM	HARD
LLYN BRIANNE & THE AFON DOETHIE	HARD
THE OLD MONKS' CHALLENGE	TOTAL MASOCHISM!

THE BIKE

THE BEST BIKE FOR YOU WILL BE THE BIKE WHICH BEST MEETS
YOUR OWN PERSONAL REQUIREMENTS. WORK OUT WHAT YOU
WANT TO DO WITH YOUR BIKE BEFORE YOU BUY. GO FOR FUNCTION
RATHER THAN FASHION (ESPECIALLY IF YOU'RE ON A TIGHT BUDGET).
TRY TO BUY SOMETHING BETTER THAN YOU NEED - SO IT WON'T HOLD
YOU BACK AS YOUR SKILLS AND FITNESS IMPROVE - BUT DON'T
BANKRUPT YOURSELF - ITS NO GOOD SPENDING A FORTUNE
IF IT MEANS YOU DON'T RIDE YOUR BIKE BECAUSE YOU'RE
SCARED OF BREAKING SOMETHING EXPENSIVE.

THE FOLLOWING LIST HAS SOME OF THE FEATURES
I'D RECOMMEND FOR RIDING THE ROUTES IN THIS BOOK.
MOST CAN BE ADDED AS UPGRADES TO ANY BASIC
MOUNTAIN BIKE.

BRAKES - POWERFUL AND CONTROLLABLE
BRAKES ARE ESSENTIAL FOR CONFIDENT RIDING.
THEY SHOULD ALSO BE EASY TO ADJUST - IF NOT
YOU WON'T BOTHER TO SET THEM UP RIGHT AND THEY'LL
NEVER WORK PROPERLY. MOST BRAKES CAN BE IMPROVED
BY FITTING GOOD QUALITY BLOCKS. BEWARE OF BLOCKS
WITH GROOVES - WHICH TRAP GRIT WHICH CAN WEAR
THROUGH THE SIDE OF YOUR RIMS.

STEM - AVAILABLE IN MANY DIFFERENT
LENGTHS AND ANGLES. IF YOU'RE NOT HAPPY
WITH YOUR HANDLEBAR POSITION AND RIDING
POSTURE TRY FITTING A DIFFERENT STEM.

SADDLE - LITERALLY A PAIN IN THE BUM
SOMETIMES. IF YOU'RE NOT COMFY TRY
A DIFFERENT ONE. MINIMALIST RACING
DESIGNS AREN'T ALWAYS THE TORTURE
IMPLEMENTS THEY APPEAR TO BE - AND THEY
GET IN THE WAY LESS WHEN YOU'RE CHUCKING YOUR WEIGHT AROUND
OUT OF THE SADDLE. SPECIAL WOMEN'S SADDLES ARE AVAILABLE -
DESIGNED FOR THE FEMALE ANATOMY.

CHAI

SPROCKE

GEARS - STEEP CLIMBS REQUIRE BIG LUNGS, POWERFUL LEGS AND
LOW GEARS. IF YOU HAVE TROUBLE RIDING UPHILL AND YOUR LOCAL BIKE
SHOP DOESN'T STOCK EXTRA LARGE THIGH MUSCLES AND LUNG
UPGRADE KITS TRY LOOKING AT YOUR LOWEST GEAR. COUNT THE

TEETH ON YOUR SMALLEST CHAINRING (FRONT) AND LARGEST SPROCKET (REAR). 24T FRONT, 28T REAR IS A TYPICAL SET UP. IF YOU HAVE 28T/28T OR AN EVEN BIGGER INNER CHAINRING YOU SHOULD CONSIDER FITTING A NEW CHAINRING AND/OR SET OF SPROCKETS. (IF YOU'VE GOT A 20T FRONT AND 32T REAR AND STILL CAN'T GET UP HILLS IT LOOKS LIKE YOU'VE RUN OUT OF EXCUSES - YOU'RE JUST GOING TO HAVE TO WORK ON THOSE LEGS AND LUNGS).

TYRES -
BIG AND KNOBBLY. FOR MOST OF THE RIDES IN THIS BOOK YOU'RE BETTER OFF SACRIFICING SMOOTH ROLLING ON TARMAC FOR MAXIMUM TRACTION OFFROAD. CHECK YOUR FRAME CLEARANCE BEFORE YOU START FITTING EXTRA LARGE TYRES - MUD CAN JAM BETWEEN THE TYRES AND FRAME OR FORKS IF YOU DON'T HAVE ENOUGH SPACE.

TYRE PRESSURE
- SOFT IS MORE COMFY AND GIVES BETTER GRIP. HIGH PRESSURE IS SMOOTHER ROLLING AND MORE PUNCTURE RESISTANT. EXPERIMENT TO FIND WHAT SUITS YOU BEST.

PEDALS -
WHETHER YOU GO FOR TOE CLIPS AND STRAPS OR 'SPD'-STYLE CLIPLESS PEDALS SOME METHOD OF FIXING YOUR FEET TO THE PEDALS WILL IMPROVE YOUR CONTROL AND LET YOU PEDAL SMOOTHLY AND EFFICIENTLY. (PRACTICE GETTING YOUR FEET IN AND OUT BEFORE YOU FIRST USE THEM IN PUBLIC!)

BAR ENDS -
LET YOU MOVE YOUR HANDS AROUND TO REDUCE FATIGUE AND GET INTO GOOD POSITIONS FOR CLIMBING AND HAMMERING ON THE FLAT.

SUSPENSION -
ADVANTAGES ARE INCREASED COMFORT AND CONTROL. DISADVANTAGES ARE COST AND WEIGHT. FRONT SUSPENSION IS NORMALLY EASY TO RETRO FIT. REAR SUSPENSION USUALLY MEANS REPLACING YOUR FRAME. WITH A GOOD SYSTEM YOU SHOULDN'T NOTICE THE SUSPENSION MOVING - YOU JUST NOTICE YOU KEEP LEAVING YOUR FRIENDS BEHIND ON THE ROUGH STUFF.

STEM

BAR END

9

THE BIKE - CONTINUED

DISPOSABLE BITS - MOUNTAIN BIKES, UNFORTUNATELY, ARE NOT INDESTRUCTIBLE. MOST COMPONENTS WILL WEAR OUT SOONER OR LATER. BRAKE CABLES, GEAR CABLES, BRAKE BLOCKS AND CHAINS ALL REQUIRE REGULAR REPLACEMENT TO KEEP YOUR BIKE SMOOTH RUNNING AND SAFE. TYRES, RIMS, CHAIN RINGS AND SPROCKETS WILL ALSO WEAR RAPIDLY IF YOU RIDE HARD. IF SOMETHING LOOKS WORN REPLACE IT - DON'T WAIT FOR IT TO BREAK 20 MILES FROM HOME!

SEALED BEARINGS & GREASEPORTS - I HATE BIKE MAINTENANCE. I'D MUCH RATHER BE OUT RIDING MY BIKE THAN SITTING AT HOME WITH IT IN BITS - SO ANYTHING THAT CUTS DOWN ON MAINTENANCE TIME MUST BE A GOOD IDEA. COMPONENTS WITH SEALED CARTRIDGE BEARINGS ARE GREAT. JUST FIT THEM AND FORGET THEM. WHEN THEY EVENTUALLY GET ROUGH JUST WHIP OUT THE BEARING CARTRIDGES AND POP IN SOME NEW ONES - EASY. UNFORTUNATELY MOST OF THESE COMPONENTS ARE NOT CHEAP. AN ALTERNATIVE IS TO GET GREASE NIPPLES FITTED TO AS MANY COMPONENTS AS POSSIBLE (ASK IN A GOOD BIKE SHOP). GET YOURSELF A GREASE GUN AND PUMP IN FRESH GREASE EVERY WEEK OR SO - YOUR COMPONENTS WILL LAST MUCH LONGER.

LIGHTWEIGHT - LIGHT BIKES ARE A GOOD IDEA - LESS WEIGHT FOR YOU TO DRAG AROUND. BUT BEWARE OF BIKES AND COMPONENTS THAT ARE TOO LIGHT - WHERE LIGHTNESS HAS BEEN ACHIEVED BY SACRIFICING PERFORMANCE OR STRENGTH. BUY LIGHT STUFF IF YOU CAN AFFORD IT - BUT REMEMBER THAT A HEAVY UNBROKEN BIKE IS A LOT BETTER THAN A LIGHT BROKEN ONE (NOT TO MENTION THE INJURIES YOU'RE LIKELY TO RECEIVE WHEN SOMETHING IMPORTANT SNAPS).

BUYING BITS - IF POSSIBLE TRY TO TAKE NEW BIKES OR COMPONENTS FOR A PROPER OFFROAD TEST RIDE BEFORE YOU BUY. IN REALITY MOST SHOPS WON'T BE TOO HAPPY ABOUT YOU DISAPPEARING FOR AN AFTERNOON WITH ONE OF THEIR BIKES OR A SET OF SHINY NEW BITS. IF YOU FANCY BUYING SOMETHING ASK OTHER PEOPLE FOR THEIR OPINIONS, LOOK FOR REVIEWS IN MAGAZINES (BUT REMEMBER THEY'RE NOT ALWAYS WRITTEN WITH YOU IN MIND), SCROUNGE RIDES ON YOUR FRIEND'S BIKES OR LOOK FOR SHOPS WITH DEMO BIKES OR HIRE BIKES WITH THE FEATURES YOU'RE INTERESTED IN. A GOOD SHOP WILL ALSO BE ABLE TO ADVISE YOU IF YOU EXPLAIN YOUR REQUIREMENTS - BUT CHECK ROUND A FEW SHOPS FOR THE BEST PRODUCTS AND SERVICE.

Tool Kit

BEST CARRIED IN A BAG FIXED TO THE BIKE — A POCKET OR
BUMBAG FULL OF TOOLS IS NOT A GOOD THING TO LAND ON IF YOU CRASH!

PUMP
— MAKE SURE IT FITS THE VALVES ON YOUR BIKE AND
TEST IT REGULARLY.

INNER TUBES
— AT LEAST ONE PER PERSON - 2 OR MORE IF
YOU'RE RIDING ALONE. ITS MUCH EASIER TO SIMPLY REPLACE
A TUBE THAN MESS AROUND TRYING TO FIX A PUNCTURE ON A
BLEAK HILLSIDE IN THE RAIN.
(CARRY A PATCH KIT AS WELL
IF YOU WANT TO BE EXTRA
CAUTIOUS). CHECK SPARE
TUBES FOR
DAMAGE
REGULARLY.

ALLEN KEYS
-3, 4, 5 & 6 MM
SHOULD DO FOR
MOST PURPOSES - BUT
CHECK ALL THE BITS
ON YOUR BIKE
TO SEE IF YOU
NEED ANY
OTHERS.

SMALL PAIR OF POINTY PLIERS
— A BIT OF A
BODGE TOOL
BUT WITH
PLENTY OF
USES WHEN
YOU'RE
DESPERATE.

6 INCH ADJUSTABLE SPANNER

TYRE LEVERS

A CHAIN TOOL MAY ALSO BE HANDY AND CHECK THE COMPONENTS
ON YOUR BIKE FOR OTHER TOOLS YOU MAY NEED.

MULTI-PURPOSE TOOLS WITH A NUMBER OF THE ABOVE FUNCTIONS
COMBINED INTO ONE TOOL CAN BE A GOOD IDEA.

LOOK AFTER YOUR BIKE
— REGULARLY SERVICE COMPONENTS AND
CHECK FOR WEAR AND DAMAGE AFTER EACH RIDE - AND YOU'LL
RARELY SUFFER FROM BREAKDOWNS.

IF YOU FIND YOU NEED TO CARRY LOADS MORE TOOLS THAN THE
ABOVE LIST YOU PROBABLY NEED TO SPEND SOME TIME
OVERHAULING YOUR BIKE INSTEAD OF RIDING IT.

11

Travelling to the Rides

Although some rides are near railway stations most people will probably travel by car. (At the time of writing the railways are being privatised so its impossible to predict the future for bikes on trains). The following list shows you some of the extra kit you should pack.

ROOFRACK OR BOOTRACK - Make sure its securely fixed and legal if you use one.

WATERPROOF GROUNDSHEET - To protect the inside of the car if you prefer to carry your bike inside.

LOCK - Make sure you're the only person who can remove your bike from your car.

BRUSH - To get the worst of the mud off your bike before you put it on, or in, the car.

SPONGE, TOWEL & BOTTLE OF WATER - To get the worst of the mud off you before you get in the car!

SPRAY LUBE - To help keep the rust monsters from eating your bike before you can get it home and clean it properly.

COMPLETE CHANGE OF CLOTHES

DEODORANT - Essential for the journey home!

SPARE FOOD & DRINK - The thought of the big bag of doughnuts waiting for you in the car will get you up the last big climb on a long hard ride.

Cleaning Your Bike

Yes I know its horrible but it has to be done - as soon as you get home. Start by removing most of the mud with a brush. Then wipe off any remaining dirt with damp rags. Mud and water can be blasted out of awkward places with lube. (Beware - some lubricants can destroy plastic seals and dissolve grease in your bearings). Avoid trying to blast the bike clean with a hose. Dry the bike and then relube all the moving bits. (Use appropriate quality products and avoid splattering them on the rims or brakes). Now reward yourself with a beer and a bath!

12

Food & Drink

Take loads - at least one bottle of water or energy drink. - 2 litres or more for long rides and in hot weather. Don't fill bottles from ponds or streams. (I was once with a group who insisted on drinking from a stream. 100 yards upstream we found the rotting remains of a dead pony lying in the water!). Take plenty of food as well. Muesli bars, chocolate, energy bars or bananas - plus butties and cakes etc if you're out over a meal time. Make sure you're well fuelled up before you set off - piles of pasta and other good carbohydrate foods the night before a ride should give you plenty to burn.

First Aid & Emergencies

First Aid Kit ⌐ Plasters, antiseptic cream, antiseptic wipes, insect bite cream, bandage & sterile dressings.
Emergency Equipment ⌐ Torch/front light, whistle (the emergency distress signal is 6 whistle blasts or torch flashes repeated every minute), LED rear light, survival bag.

This is far too complex a subject to cover in detail here - but these are some of the basics. Trailside first aid - like trailside bike repairs - should be treated as a temporary fix. Get yourself home and get it dealt with properly - seek medical attention if necessary. Make sure your tetanus jabs are up to date or even small cuts could become serious.

Most emergencies are caused by over exertion or crashes. Look for tiredness, moodiness and erratic behaviour - possible signs of hypothermia, dehydration or heat exhaustion. Rest, eat, drink and warm them if they're cold. If someone is injured the priorities are to check their breathing and stop any bleeding (apply pressure to the wound - never try tourniquets). Then get them off the hills and to safety. If the casualty can't be moved make them comfortable and leave food, (avoid drink unless they're dehydrated), spare clothes and at least one person with them. Make certain you know their exact location on the map and head for the nearest help.

Before you set off on a ride always make sure someone knows where you're going and when you should be back.

13

THE WELL DRESSED MOUNTAIN BIKER — SUMMER

HELMET - ESSENTIAL FOR SERIOUS OFFROAD RIDING

SHADES - NOT JUST FOR POSING - THEY KEEP INSECTS, GRIT AND DOG CRAP OUT OF YOUR EYES

CYCLING MITTS - EXTRA PADDING FOR YOUR HANDS, PROTECT YOUR KNUCKLES FROM BRAMBLES AND STOP SWEATY HANDS SLIPPING OFF THE BARS.

T-SHIRT OR CYCLING SHIRT

BUMBAG WITH LONG SLEEVED TOP - IN CASE IT GETS CHILLY

CYCLING SHORTS - BY FAR THE COMFIEST THING TO WEAR NEXT TO YOUR TENDER BITS

MTB SHOES OR LIGHTWEIGHT HIKING BOOTS - A FAIRLY STIFF SOLE IS BEST FOR CYCLING BUT YOU'LL ALSO NEED SOMETHING WITH GOOD GRIP AND A BIT OF FLEX FOR WALKING. REMEMBER - YOU'LL BE WALKING WHERE THE GROUND CONDITIONS ARE TOO EXTREME FOR CYCLING - MAKE SURE YOUR FOOTWEAR IS SUITABLE FOR THESE CONDITIONS

TRY TO WORK OUT A SYSTEM FOR JUDGING HOW MUCH YOU NEED TO WEAR. I FIND IF I'M SLIGHTLY COLD BEFORE STARTING I'M DRESSED ABOUT RIGHT - I SOON WARM UP TO A COMFY RIDING TEMPERATURE - NOT TOO HOT ON THE CLIMBS OR TOO COLD ON DESCENTS

GORE TEX HELMET COVER OR THIN BALACLAVA BENEATH YOUR HELMET

CLEAR SHADES - KEEP MUD ETC OUT OF YOUR EYES

GLOVES - MAKE SURE THEY'RE WARM, WINDPROOF AND DON'T RESTRICT YOUR FINGERS WORKING THE CONTROLS

THERMAL BASE LAYER - A PROPER BASE LAYER SHIRT WILL WICK MOISTURE AWAY FROM YOUR SKIN - YOU'LL SWEAT EVEN ON THE COLDEST DAYS. IF SWEAT STAYS NEXT TO YOUR SKIN IT'LL SOON COOL AND START TO CHILL YOU

BUM BAG WITH EXTRA TOP AND WATERPROOF JACKET

MID LAYERS - FLEECE IS IDEAL - MIX AND MATCH LAYERS ACCORDING TO THE WEATHER

TROUSERS - STRETCHY TO ALLOW MUSCLE MOVEMENT. A FAIRLY TIGHT FIT WILL STOP THE LEGS FROM FLAPPING IN THE CHAIN AND THE CROTCH FROM CATCHING ON THE BACK OF THE SADDLE WHEN YOU'RE HANGING OFF THE BACK ON A STEEP DESCENT. WEAR YOUR CYCLING SHORTS UNDERNEATH

WINDPROOF OUTER LAYER - A GARMENT DESIGNED SPECIALLY FOR CYCLING WILL GIVE THE BEST FIT. A HIGH COLLAR, LONG FRONT ZIP AND ELASTICATED CUFFS ALLOW YOU TO CONTROL YOUR BODY TEMPERATURE

WATERPROOF BOOTS

SOCKS - A COUPLE OF WARM PAIRS - BUT DON'T OVERDO IT - IF YOUR FEET ARE SQUEEZED IN YOUR BOOTS IT'LL RESTRICT YOUR CIRCULATION AND YOUR FEET WILL GET COLD QUICKER **15**

How To Ride

This is far too big a subject to cover in detail here - but here are a few basic tips which may help you improve your riding.

UP

WEIGHT OVER REAR WHEEL FOR MAXIMUM TRACTION

BALANCE

- Riding on the flat you should be perfectly balanced - your weight evenly spaced between the wheels. Weight over the front wheel helps steering and braking. Weight on the rear helps braking and traction. But riding offroad rarely involves riding on the flat - so you need to move your body around if you're going to stay balanced.

GOING UP. - On steep climbs get into a lowish gear and spin the pedals smooth and fast. Sit forward on the nose of the saddle or stand with your bum directly above the seat. You need to stop the front wheel from lifting off the ground - but also keep most of your weight back for maximum rear wheel traction.

GOING DOWN. - Stand with your bum above the back of the saddle and use your arms and legs as shock absorbers. If its really steep move your weight right back (dropping the saddle helps). But don't go too far - if you try to hide behind your back wheel you'll just lose control of the front end.

ROCKS & LOGS - Sometimes it helps to deliberately unbalance the bike. By throwing your weight back you'll lighten the front wheel allowing it to roll up onto an obstacle. Throw your weight forward and the back wheel will roll up as well. (Take this a stage further and you can use wheelies and hops to get over big obstacles in style).

DOWN

WEIGHT BACK TO BALANCE BOTH WHEELS AND STOP YOU GOING OVER THE FRONT

MOMENTUM

A bit of speed will often carry you through trouble far better than slowing down. A fast bike can skim smoothly over the tops of bumps — whereas if you slow down the wheels will drop down into the dips and you'll get a much rougher ride.

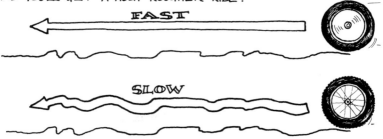

FAST

SLOW

If you go too slow you'll also lose your balance and wobble — further reducing your chance of riding an obstacle.

VERY STEEP DROPS - the two things to check for are a straight line down and a smooth flat run out at the bottom. Then go for it — let yourself roll and don't touch the brakes until you reach the run out area. Don't brake on the way down — if its very steep gravity's going to get you to the bottom whatever you do. Your brakes won't stop you — they'll just make you skid and lose control and you'll end up sliding down on your bum. Concentrate on keeping the wheels rolling in a straight line beneath you until you reach flat ground where you can stop. (This can be seriously scary at first — but big fun when you get the hang of it).

ANTICIPATION

Obvious really - don't just look ahead — think ahead as well. Look for the best line, be ready to brake or change gear when you need to. Always ride within the limits of what you can see — tracks can have all sorts of nasties hiding round the next bend. Even if you know the track it can still be hazardous. These are some of the dangers I've found lurking round bends on some of my favourite downhills :- sheep, dead sheep, horses, walkers, tractors, herd of cattle, BMW (with the occupants getting very friendly on the back seat!) lorry exhaust pipe, newly dug ditch, fallen tree, wooden bridge with planks missing, film crew filming a historical drama (honest!).

17

How to Ride - continued

PRACTICE

You'll never be any good if you don't practice, and even experienced riders can learn new things and develop existing skills. Never let yourself think 'I can't do that' if something really is too scary find something similar but easier elsewhere and try that. Get confident and then go back and have another crack at the big one. If you make mistakes - learn from them and try not to make them again. Its worth going out just to play sometimes - (it doesn't matter if you're 14 or 40! - wear old clothes and take some friends. Don't try new skills alone or anywhere remote). Find somewhere soft and push yourself to the limits- and beyond (yes its good to practice crashing as well ! Knowing when and how to abandon ship may just save some skin one day). Practice and you'll boost your confidence and skills, making your riding more enjoyable.

EROSION

A sensible mountain biker should cause no more damage than a sensible walker. So how sensible are you ? The most important rule is don't skid. If the only way you can ride a piece of terrain involves ripping it up - don't ride it, get off and walk. Some surfaces are obviously fragile - be aware of the damage you could cause and try to leave no marks to tell others where you've been. Where trails are already damaged you'll have to decide for yourself what seems best - go through the middle, potentially making things worse - or go round, possibly spreading the erosion over a wider area. If you find that trails are damaged or can't be ridden because they're blocked or overgrown, why not do something about it. Contact the local authority's rights of way officer and volunteer to help.

GROUP RIDING

Never leave anyone behind and never push anyone to ride too fast or to do something if they don't want to. Ride at your own pace - but if you're faster than others stop regularly to regroup. Make sure everyone gets enough rest before you set off again. Take turns to play tail-end Charlie. Learn from watching other riders. (But don't follow them blindly - if they crash so will you). 4 or 5 riders is an ideal number on remote rides. If someone has an accident at least one person can stay with them while 2 go for help.

THE MOUNTAIN BIKE & COUNTRY CODES

ENJOY THE COUNTRYSIDE AND RESPECT ITS LIFE AND WORK

ONLY RIDE WHERE
YOU KNOW YOU
HAVE A LEGAL
RIGHT

ALWAYS GIVE WAY TO HORSES AND WALKERS

AVOID ANIMALS, CROPS AND MACHINERY

TAKE ALL LITTER HOME WITH YOU

LEAVE ALL GATES AS FOUND

DON'T GET ANNOYED WITH ANYONE - IT NEVER SOLVES PROBLEMS

ALWAYS TRY TO BE
SELF-SUFFICIENT - FOR
YOU AND YOUR BIKE

NEVER CREATE A FIRE HAZARD

KEEP YOUR DOGS UNDER CLOSE CONTROL

USE GATES AND
STILES TO CROSS
FENCES, HEDGES
AND WALLS

HELP KEEP ALL WATER CLEAN

PROTECT WILDLIFE, PLANTS AND TREES

TAKE SPECIAL CARE ON COUNTRY ROADS

MAKE NO
UNNECESSARY
NOISE

ANIMALS & PEOPLE

WILD ANIMALS

WILD ANIMALS – THERE ARE VIRTUALLY NO DANGEROUS WILD CREATURES IN BRITAIN. THE ADDER HAS A VENOMOUS BITE WHICH CAN BE VERY PAINFUL – BUT IT IS RARELY LIFE THREATENING. YOU'RE EXTREMELY UNLIKELY TO EVER SEE ONE – AND UNLESS YOU DISGUISE YOURSELF AS A SMALL VOLE OR DO SOMETHING STUPID LIKE TREAD ON IT – YOU'RE EVEN LESS LIKELY TO GET BITTEN. MOST WILD ANIMALS ARE FAR MORE SCARED OF YOU THAN YOU ARE OF THEM.

WHO SAYS WILD ANIMALS AIN'T DANGEROUS?

SHEEP

SHEEP – BASICALLY SHEEP ARE COMPLETELY STUPID. IF THEY CAN GET IN YOUR WAY THEN THEY WILL. DON'T BOTHER TRYING TO WORK OUT WHAT A SHEEP IS ABOUT TO DO – THE SHEEP DOESN'T KNOW SO HOW CAN YOU KNOW? AVOID SCARING SHEEP AND NEVER CHASE THEM – IF LAMBS GET SEPARATED FROM THEIR MOTHERS THEY CAN BE ABANDONED AND DIE AND IF YOU FRIGHTEN PREGNANT EWES THEY COULD MISCARRY.

CATTLE

CATTLE – COWS ARE USUALLY PRETTY PASSIVE. YOU'RE UNLIKELY TO MEET MANY BULLS AND IF YOU DO THEY SHOULD ALSO BE DOCILE – BEST TO GIVE THEM A WIDE BERTH ANYWAY. BULLOCKS AND HEIFERS ARE OFTEN VERY INQUISITIVE WHICH CAN BE INTIMIDATING – BUT SHOUT 'BOO' AND THEY'LL USUALLY RUN AWAY. AVOID STAMPEDING CATTLE.

DOGS

DOGS – BY FAR THE MOST DANGEROUS ANIMALS YOU'RE LIKELY TO MEET. ALL DOGS SHOULD BE TREATED WITH EXTREME CAUTION. THE DANGERS OF THE TEETH AND CLAWS ARE ALL TOO OBVIOUS – BUT WATCH OUT ALSO FOR STUPID DOGS THAT RUN IN FRONT OF YOU AND CAN KNOCK YOU OFF. IF YOU HAVE PROBLEMS WITH DOGS (ESPECIALLY FARM DOGS) YOU SHOULD REPORT THEM TO THE LOCAL AUTHORITY'S RIGHTS OF WAY OFFICER. IF YOU ARE ATTACKED OR INJURED BY A DOG

MAN'S BEST FRIEND?

YOU SHOULD REPORT IT TO THE POLICE. BEWARE ALSO OF DOG CRAP. IF YOU GET IT ON YOUR SKIN - WASH IT OFF AS QUICKLY AND THOROUGHLY AS POSSIBLE. IF IT GETS ON YOUR FACE ITS SENSIBLE TO SEEK MEDICAL ADVICE. IF YOU GET IT ON YOUR WATER BOTTLE DON'T DRINK FROM IT - TAKE IT HOME AND BIN IT.

HORSE RIDERS – ALWAYS GIVE WAY TO HORSES AND NEVER
FRIGHTEN THEM. IF A HORSE PANICS IT COULD INJURE BOTH THE RIDER AND YOU.

NEXT PUB
50 MILES

YOU CAN'T EXPECT WALKERS TO SMILE ALL OF THE TIME!

WALKERS – IT'S A WELL KNOWN MYTH
THAT WALKERS AND MOUNTAIN BIKERS HATE EACH OTHER. IN REALITY THIS IS RARELY THE CASE. MOUNTAIN BIKERS AND WALKERS HAVE A LOT IN COMMON AND HAVE MUCH TO BENEFIT FROM COOPERATING WITH EACH OTHER. MOST SENSIBLE PEOPLE REALISE THIS. GIVE WAY TO THOSE ON FOOT AND BE POLITE AND FRIENDLY AND YOU'LL RARELY HAVE ANY PROBLEMS. AVOID CONFRONTATION WITH ANYONE - IT GETS YOU NOWHERE.

LANDOWNERS – THE SHOTGUN WIELDING FARMER YELLING
'GEDORFF MY LAAAND' IS ANOTHER MYTH. MOST PEOPLE ARE PERFECTLY HAPPY TO LET YOU RIDE ACROSS THEIR LAND AS LONG AS YOU STICK TO THE RIGHTS OF WAY AND RESPECT THEIR PROPERTY AND WORK. MOST FARMERS ARE PRETTY FRIENDLY IF YOU STOP FOR A CHAT (IT CAN LEAD TO SOME INTERESTING SITUATIONS TOO - LIKE HELPING TO ROUND UP SHEEP ON YOUR BIKE, OR BEING CHALLENGED TO AN INFORMAL TRIALS COMPETITION BY A SHEPHERD ON A MOTOCROSS BIKE. YOU CAN ALSO SOMETIMES GET PERMISSION TO RIDE ON PRIVATE TRACKS).

ITS ALWAYS WORTH BEING FRIENDLY TO FARMERS!

21

Useful Contacts

Tourist Information Centres — FOR DETAILS OF ACCOMMODATION, CAFÉS AND OFF-BIKE ACTIVITIES.

ABERYSTWYTH - TERRACE ROAD, ABERYSTWYTH, SY23 2AG. TEL: 01970 612125.

BALA - PENLLYN, PENSARN ROAD, BALA, LL23 7SR. TEL: 01678 521021.

CHURCH STRETTON - THE LIBRARY, CHURCH STREET, CHURCH STRETTON. 01694 723133.

DOLGELLAU - TY MEIRION, ELDON SQUARE, DOLGELLAU, LL40 1PU. TEL: 01341 422888.

IRONBRIDGE - 4 THE WHARFAGE, IRONBRIDGE, TF8 7AW. TEL: 01952 432166.

KINGTON - MILL STREET, KINGTON, HEREFORD + WORCESTER. TEL: 01544 230778.

KNIGHTON - OFFA'S DYKE CENTRE, WEST STREET, KNIGHTON, LD7 1EN. TEL: 01547 528753.

LLANDRINDOD WELLS - OLD TOWN HALL, MEMORIAL GARDENS, LLANDRINDOD WELLS, LD1 5DL.
TEL: 01597 822600.

LLANGOLLEN - TOWN HALL, CASTLE STREET, LLANGOLLEN, LL20 5PD. TEL: 01978 860828.

LLANIDLOES - THE TOWN HALL, GREAT OAK STREET, LLANIDLOES, SY18 6BN. TEL: 01686 412605.

LUDLOW - CASTLE STREET, LUDLOW, SY8 1AF. TEL: 01584 875053.

MACHYNLLETH - CANOLFAN OWAIN GLYNDŴR, MACHYNLLETH, SY20 8EE. TEL: 01654 702401.

NEWTOWN - CENTRAL CAR PARK, NEWTOWN, SY16 2PW. TEL: 01686 625580.

SHREWSBURY - THE SQUARE, SHREWSBURY, SY1 1LH. TEL 01743 350761

WELSHPOOL - VICARAGE GARDEN CAR PARK, WELSHPOOL, SY21 7DD. TEL: 01938 552043.

THESE ARE THE MAIN ONES, MOSTLY OPEN ALL YEAR. MANY OTHER TOWNS AND VILLAGES ALSO HAVE CENTRES, OPEN IN THE SUMMER ONLY.

Rights of Way Officers — IF YOU HAVE ANY RIGHTS OF WAY PROBLEMS OR QUERIES.

CEREDIGION COUNTY COUNCIL - HIGHWAYS, PROPERTY + WORKS DEPT, COUNTY HALL, MARKET STREET, ABERAERON, SA46 0AT.

DENBIGHSHIRE COUNTY COUNCIL - HIGHWAYS + TRANSPORTATION DEPT, COUNTY HALL, MOLD, CH7 6GU.

GWYNEDD COUNTY COUNCIL - HIGHWAYS + ENGINEERING DEPT, SWYDDFA ARDAL MEIRIONNYDD, CAE PENARLÂG, DOLGELLAU, GWYNEDD, LL40 2YB.

HEREFORD + WORCESTER COUNTY COUNCIL - ENVIRONMENTAL SERVICES DEPT, COUNTY HALL, SPETCHLEY RD, WORCESTER, WR5 2NP.

POWYS COUNTY COUNCIL - RIGHTS OF WAY SECTION, COUNTY HALL, LLANDRINDOD WELLS, POWYS, LD1 5LG.

SHROPSHIRE COUNTY COUNCIL - COUNTRYSIDE SERVICE, COLUMN HOUSE, 7 LONDON ROAD, SHREWSBURY, SY2 6NW.

WREXHAM COUNTY BOROUGH - HIGHWAYS + TRANSPORTATION SERVICES DEPT, CROWN BUILDINGS, PO BOX 1293, WREXHAM, LL11 1WQ.

OTHER ORGANISATIONS

CYCLISTS TOURING CLUB - COTTERELL HOUSE, 69 MEADROW, GODALMING, SURREY, GU7 3HS.

DŴR CWMRU / WELSH WATER - ELAN VALLEY ESTATE OFFICE, RHAYADER, POWYS, SY16 2AB.

FOREST ENTERPRISE DISTRICT OFFICES :-
    CEREDIGION - LLANAFAN, ABERYSTWYTH, SY23 4AY.
    DOLGELLAU - ARRAN ROAD, DOLGELLAU, GWYNEDD, LL40 1LW.
    LLANDOVERY - LLANFAIR ROAD, LLANDOVERY, SA20 0AL.
    LLANRWST (NORTH WALES) - GWYDYR UCHAF, LLANRWST, LL26 0PN.
    MARCHES - WHITCLIFFE, LUDLOW, SHROPSHIRE, SY8 2HD.
    NEWTOWN - ST DAVID'S HOUSE, NEWTOWN, POWYS, SY16 1RB.
NATIONAL TRUST (MERCIA REGION) - ATTINGHAM PARK, SHREWSBURY, SY4 4TP.
SNOWDONIA NATIONAL PARK - PENRHYNDEUDRAETH, GWYNEDD, LL48 6LF.
SUSTRANS - 35 KING STREET, BRISTOL, BS1 4DZ.
WREKIN COUNCIL - CIVIC OFFICES, P.O. BOX 211, TELFORD, TF3 4LA.

WEATHER FORECASTS

BAD WEATHER CAN TURN A GENTLE AFTERNOON RIDE INTO A TOTAL NIGHTMARE. WIND, RAIN AND COLD CAN MAKE THINGS REALLY HORRIBLE AND MIST WILL MAKE NAVIGATION VERY DIFFICULT. (BEWARE ALSO OF EXTREMELY HOT WEATHER.) ON EXPOSED ROUTES EXTREME CONDITIONS CAN BE LIFE THREATENING! WEATHER CAN CHANGE VERY QUICKLY IN THE HILLS. JUST BECAUSE IT WAS NICE WHEN YOU SET OFF IT DOESN'T MEAN IT WILL STAY THAT WAY ALL DAY. LISTEN TO WEATHER FORECASTS ON LOCAL RADIO OR TV BEFORE SETTING OFF. IF YOU'RE HEADING INTO SNOWDONIA YOU CAN GET A DETAILED RECORDED FORECAST FOR THE AREA ON **0891 500 449**. IF IT'S GOING TO BE HORRIBLE FORGET ABOUT SETTING OFF ON SOME EPIC EXPEDITION AND CHOOSE A NICE SHELTERED ROUTE INSTEAD (VALLEYS AND FORESTS ARE GOOD).

ROUTE MAINTENANCE

MID-WALES AND THE MARCHES HAVE THOUSANDS OF MILES OF BRIDLEWAYS AND OTHER RIGHTS OF WAY WHICH IN THEORY CAN BE USED BY MOUNTAIN BIKERS. BUT IN REALITY YOU'LL FIND THAT MANY TRACKS ARE BLOCKED OR HAVE SIMPLY VANISHED THROUGH LACK OF USE. SO WHY NOT DO SOMETHING ABOUT IT? CONTACT THE RIGHTS OF WAY PEOPLE AT YOUR LOCAL AUTHORITY AND ASK IF THEY'VE GOT ANY PATH MAINTENANCE SCHEMES FOR VOLUNTEERS. THE WORK CAN BE GOOD FUN, YOU GET A SENSE OF SATISFACTION FROM PUTTING SOMETHING BACK INTO THE COUNTRYSIDE AND (BEST OF ALL) YOU GET SOME GOOD CLEAR TRACKS TO RIDE.

Riding around Dolgellau and Corris is a bit like riding through a geography textbook. During the ice age glaciers ripped through the landscape leaving classic steep sided, flat bottomed valleys and towering, craggy peaks.

This route loops around Corris, through some of Snowdonia's most dramatic scenery. There are some long climbs over mountain passes - rewarded with brilliant descents down the far side.

If you fancy trying a shorter version of this route - leave out the Dolgellau leg and just ride the 13½ mile (22km) loop around Corris. Start from the car park at the top of the pass 753 135.

CORRIS

MAP: Landranger 124 or Outdoor Leisure 23
DISTANCE: 20½ miles /33 km   OFFROAD: 9 miles /14km
TIME: 2½ - 4½ hours
HIGHEST POINT: 1300ft /400m
TOTAL CLIMBING: 3700ft /1130m
START: Dolgellau   728 177

From the centre of Dolgellau take the road heading east out of town. Near the hospital turn right up a road named 'Fron Serth' and after 400 yards turn right again. This little road becomes a steep climb above a picturesque tree-lined stream. Bear left after ¾ mile (1km) and keep climbing until you eventually reach the end of the road. Go straight on - over a stile and up a couple of tiny fields. By a stone shed turn left and scramble up a

24

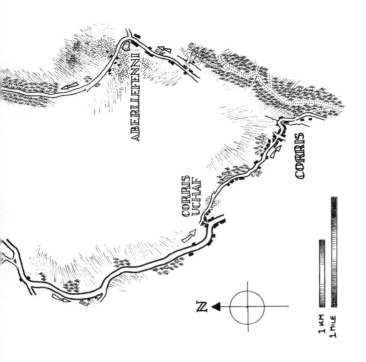

ABERLLEFENNI

CORRIS UCHAF

CORRIS

N

1 KM
1 MILE

ROUGH, TREE-LINED PATH. THROUGH A GATE THE PATH SWINGS RIGHT AND FOLLOWS A WALL
ALONG THE BOTTOM OF AN OVERGROWN FIELD. AFTER GOING THROUGH A GAP IN AN
OLD WALL YOU CROSS ALMOST TO THE FAR SIDE OF A FIELD AND THEN TURN LEFT
(SWINGING BACK ON YOURSELF A BIT) AND CLIMB A FAINT PATH TO THE TOP OF THE FIELD.
CLIMB OVER A STILE AND FOLLOW THE FAINT PATH UP OVER THE BROW OF THE HILL
(A SPUR OF CADAIR IDRIS WHICH RISES DRAMATICALLY TO YOUR RIGHT).

OVER THE BROW SWING RIGHT AND CONTINUE ALONG THE FAINT PATH, TWISTING AND
BUMPING DOWN TO A GATE IN A CORNER. GO THROUGH AND, KEEPING THE WALL
(LATER FENCE) ON YOUR LEFT, CONTINUE AROUND THE HILLSIDE, THROUGH VARIOUS
GATES FOR 3/4 MILE (1KM). EVENTUALLY YOU REACH A SMALL TRIANGULAR FENCED AREA
NEAR A TRACK THROUGH A FORD. SWING RIGHT TO A LITTLE MARKER POST AND
THEN FOLLOW THE BANK OF THE STREAM DOWN TO THE FORD. BEYOND THE FORD THE
WIDE TRACK NARROWS, AND AFTER 1/2 MILE (0.75KM) FINALLY LEADS YOU TO
A ROAD.

Turn right on the main road. After a short, gentle climb you reach the top of the pass and a fantastic view opens up - with huge crags and cliffs stretching up on either side and the ground dropping away in front of you down towards Talyllyn Lake. 300 yards after passing a layby/car park look for a gate on the right. Go through and you find yourself on the old road DOWN the pass - now a brilliant smooth, grassy track. Swoop down into the valley. The track eventually becomes tarmac and rejoins the main road.

Shortly the road begins gently climbing again - over another pass. ½ mile (0.7 km) of gentle descent on the far side brings you to Corris Uchaf where you turn left on a minor road down to Corris. At a steep crossroads go straight across and drop down to a bridge over a river. Beyond the bridge follow the road along the bottom of a forest, until 200 yards after passing a large forest track, bear left up a narrow track. Climb up through the trees until you reach a large track and turn left. After ½ mile (0.8 km) bear left at a fork and then after the same distance again, turn left onto a narrow path by a small waymarker post. After a few wiggles this becomes a gorgeous little straight, narrow descent (watch out for a couple of little ditches. - not major hazards, but they were enough to launch me over the bars!). When you reach a gate go through and follow the track along the bottom edge of the forest. Go left at a junction, down to a bridge and then up to the road beyond.

Turn right and cruise along the tarmac to Aberllefenni. The remains of the valley's old slate industry still dominate the village. The scars of old quarries are etched into the hillsides and the abandoned buildings, inclines and machinery give a fascinating insight into a bygone era in this now sleepy community. Follow the road up the valley to the left, past the quarry ruins. After 1½ miles (2.5 km) you climb up to the end of the road. Take the right-hand track and continue upwards, past a ruined farm and up a steep, rocky slog until you finally haul yourself up out of the end of the valley.

After a couple of minutes rest its time for the descent - 1 mile (1.5 km) of smooth, fast grassy blast (watch out for gates) back down to the A487. When you reach the main road turn left and climb gently for ¾ mile (1 km) until you reach the gate at the end of the track from Dolgellau. Turn onto the track and carefully retrace the first part of the route all the way back to the start.

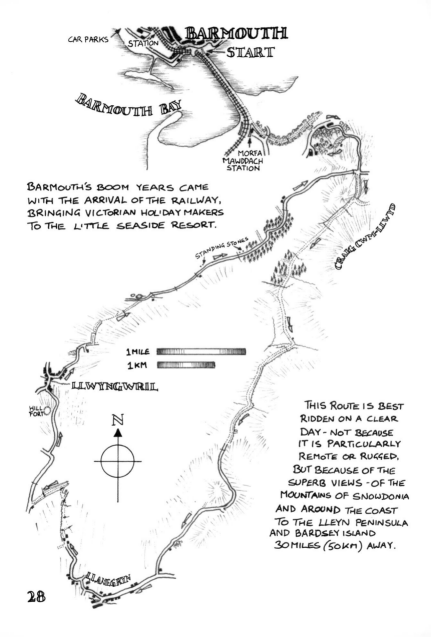

CAR PARKS STATION **BARMOUTH START**

BARMOUTH BAY

MORFA MAWDDACH STATION

BARMOUTH'S BOOM YEARS CAME WITH THE ARRIVAL OF THE RAILWAY, BRINGING VICTORIAN HOLIDAY MAKERS TO THE LITTLE SEASIDE RESORT.

STANDING STONES

CRAIG CWM-LLWYD

1 MILE
1 KM

LLWYNGWRIL

HILL FORT

N

THIS ROUTE IS BEST RIDDEN ON A CLEAR DAY - NOT BECAUSE IT IS PARTICULARLY REMOTE OR RUGGED, BUT BECAUSE OF THE SUPERB VIEWS - OF THE MOUNTAINS OF SNOWDONIA AND AROUND THE COAST TO THE LLEYN PENINSULA AND BARDSEY ISLAND 30 MILES (50 KM) AWAY.

LLANEGRYN

BARMOUTH COAST ROUTE 2

MAP: LANDRANGER 124 OR OUTDOOR LEISURE 23
DISTANCE: 24 MILES / 38.5 KM   OFFROAD: 11 MILES / 17.5 KM
TIME: 2½ - 3½ HOURS
HIGHEST POINT: 1300FT / 400M   (BUT YOU START FROM SEA LEVEL!)
TOTAL CLIMBING: 3100 FT / 950 M
START: END OF RAILWAY BRIDGE, BARMOUTH   619 155

FROM THE CENTRE OF TOWN GO EAST ALONG THE MAIN ROAD. AT THE TOP OF
A SHORT SLOPE TURN RIGHT ONTO A TARMAC PATH DOWN TO THE END OF
THE RAILWAY BRIDGE. (THERE IS A SMALL TOLL CHARGE SO MAKE SURE YOU'VE
GOT SOME MONEY). CROSS THE BRIDGE AND FOLLOW THE SANDY PATH BESIDE
THE RAILWAY TO MORFA MAWDDACH STATION. PASS THE DERELICT PLATFORM
AND FOLLOW THE PATH TO A GATE. GO THROUGH ONTO THE ROUTE OF THE DISMANTLED
RAILWAY TO DOLGELLAU. AFTER A FEW HUNDRED YARDS GO THROUGH ANOTHER
GATE AND AFTER ⅓ MILE (0.5 KM) YOU COME TO A THIRD ONE. DON'T GO THROUGH
THIS GATE BUT TURN RIGHT ONTO A TRACK LEADING TO THE ROAD.

TURN LEFT ON THE ROAD THEN RIGHT UP A VERY STEEP MINOR ROAD IN THE
MIDDLE OF A ROW OF HOUSES. THE LOWER PART OF THIS CLIMB IS
WOODED BUT AS YOU GET HIGHER YOU FIND EXCELLENT VIEWS OF BARMOUTH
OPENING UP BEHIND YOU (A GOOD EXCUSE TO STOP FOR A REST!). KEEP
CLIMBING, GOING THROUGH A GATE AND PAST A FARM UNTIL YOU REACH A
JUNCTION. YOU WILL RETURN TO THIS POINT LATER IN THE RIDE - SO YOU
CAN CHOOSE TO DO THE ROUTE EITHER CLOCKWISE OR ANTICLOCKWISE.
ANTICLOCKWISE GIVES BETTER OFFROAD DESCENTS - BUT I SHALL
DESCRIBE IT CLOCKWISE WHICH GIVES EASIER CLIMBS AND FACES THE BEST VIEWS.

GO STRAIGHT AHEAD AT THE JUNCTION UP A WALLED TRACK. GO THROUGH
THE GATE AT THE TOP AND CONTINUE STRAIGHT AHEAD. THE TRACK SKIRTS
ALONG THE HILLSIDE BELOW THE CRAGS OF CRAIG CWM-LLWYD WITH
BRILLIANT VIEWS UP THE COAST OPENING OUT ON THE RIGHT. CONTINUE ALONG
THE CLEAR TRACK, THROUGH VARIOUS GATES, FOR ABOUT 3½ MILES (6 KM).
THE TRACK EVENTUALLY BECOMES A SMALL ROAD THAT DROPS STEEPLY
INTO THE VALLEY OF THE AFON DYSYNNI.

TURN RIGHT AT THE T-JUNCTION AND RIDE ALONG THE ROAD FOR ¾ MILE
(1KM) INTO THE QUIET VILLAGE OF LLANEGRYN. TURN RIGHT BY THE BRIDGE
AND RIGHT AGAIN AFTER 400 YARDS. LEFT AFTER ANOTHER 300 YARDS
AND THEN AFTER ¾ MILE (1KM) GO STRAIGHT AHEAD INTO A FARMYARD.
PASS THE FARMHOUSE AND THEN RIDE ROUND TO THE LEFT OF A BARN AND
CLIMB UP A ROCK AND COWPAT COVERED TRACK BESIDE A STREAM. GO

29

Through the gate at the top of the track and turn right along the wall until you come to another gate on your right. Ignore the gate and turn left up the field. At the top of the field go through a gate or over a ladder stile. Do the same at the top of the next field and continue up a third field until you can turn left into the adjacent field. Keep going upwards, round the outside of the small field with the ruined barn, until you reach another gate and stile leading into a walled green lane. (This is all a lot easier than it sounds. Basically you just keep heading upwards and look for the ladder stiles as landmarks). Turn left on the green lane and follow it for ½ mile (0.75 km) to a road by a ruined farm. Turn right on the tarmac and roll along admiring the brilliant views. At a junction turn right and take the road down the hill - looking out for cattle grids, and the remains of Castell y Gaer hillfort on your left.

At the t-junction turn right into Llwyngwril. Over the bridge turn right by the pub and follow a little road as it climbs steadily for approx ¾ mile (1km). Where the road turns sharp right to a farm continue straight ahead up a steep grassy track. After a short distance the track turns left and climbs more gently across the hillside. The route is mostly pretty clear. Follow the track, through a few gates, and onto a small gated road by a pond. Turn right (effectively straight on) along the road. After passing through a gate by some sheep pens and a caravan, look in the field on your left where you can see some prehistoric standing stones. More can be seen by the roadside further on where you enter a forest. After the forest the road takes you into an amazing landscape of jumbled crags and rock outcrops before dropping down to the junction where you made your clockwise or anticlockwise choice.

Turn left back down the road. After going through the gate continue to a sharp right bend and go straight ahead onto a bridleway. Follow the grassy lane past a cottage in a field on your left and then turn right to go past the side of another cottage. The track then narrows and zig zags steeply down through a wood. Ignore paths off to either side and let gravity guide you straight down until you emerge on a road. Turn right and then right again on the main road. Just round the bend turn left onto the track back to the old railway. Left again - back to the bridge and across to Barmouth, where you can reward your efforts with a paddle in the sea and a huge ice cream!

Barmouth Bridge ▶

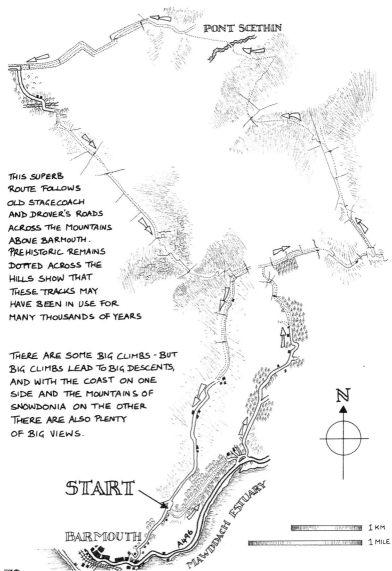

PONT SCETHIN

THIS SUPERB
ROUTE FOLLOWS
OLD STAGECOACH
AND DROVER'S ROADS
ACROSS THE MOUNTAINS
ABOVE BARMOUTH.
PREHISTORIC REMAINS
DOTTED ACROSS THE
HILLS SHOW THAT
THESE TRACKS MAY
HAVE BEEN IN USE FOR
MANY THOUSANDS OF YEARS

THERE ARE SOME BIG CLIMBS - BUT
BIG CLIMBS LEAD TO BIG DESCENTS,
AND WITH THE COAST ON ONE
SIDE AND THE MOUNTAINS OF
SNOWDONIA ON THE OTHER
THERE ARE ALSO PLENTY
OF BIG VIEWS.

N

START

BARMOUTH

A496

MAWDDACH ESTUARY

1 KM

1 MILE

Pont Scethin

MAP: LANDRANGER 124 OR OUTDOOR LEISURE 18
DISTANCE: 17½ MILES / 28 KM   OFFROAD: 13¾ MILES / 22 KM
TIME: 3-5½ HOURS
HIGHEST POINT: 1830 FT / 560 M
TOTAL CLIMBING: 3300 FT / 1000 M
START: CAR PARK ON MINOR ROAD ABOVE BARMOUTH   625 166

STARTING FROM THE LITTLE CAR PARK, TRUNDLE BACK DOWN THE ROAD FOR A
FEW YARDS THEN TURN LEFT THROUGH A GATE WITH A SIGN FOR THE 'PANORAMA
WALK'. FOLLOW THE TRACK AROUND A ROCKY LITTLE HILL AND INTO A WOOD. GO
THROUGH A GATE AND THEN CONTINUE STRAIGHT ON DOWN THE TRACK (DON'T
TURN RIGHT THROUGH ANOTHER 'PANORAMA WALK' GATE). TAKE IT GENTLY DOWN HERE,
WATCHING OUT FOR WALKERS. FOLLOW THE TRACK ALL THE WAY DOWN THROUGH THE
WOOD AND CONTINUE STRAIGHT ON DOWNWARDS WHEN YOU EMERGE ONTO A SMALL
ROAD. TURN LEFT AT THE BOTTOM, PAST SOME IMPRESSIVE-LOOKING GARDENS,
AND THEN, JUST BEFORE MEETING THE MAIN ROAD, TURN LEFT UP ANOTHER MINOR ROAD.
FOLLOW THIS ROAD STEADILY UPWARDS FOR 1½ MILES (2.5 KM). EVENTUALLY THE
TARMAC ENDS AND YOU CONTINUE STRAIGHT ON ALONG A GRASSY TRACK BETWEEN
A WALL AND A FOREST. FOLLOW THE TRACK ALONG THE FOREST EDGE AND THEN
BEAR RIGHT INTO A FIELD AT THE END. CONTINUE ALONG THE CLEARLY VISIBLE
TRACK INTO ANOTHER FIELD, THROUGH A SMALL FORD AND THEN UP TO A TRACK
JUNCTION.

TURN RIGHT AND FOLLOW THE WELL DEFINED TRACK PAST THE TOP OF THE FOREST
AND AROUND THE HILLSIDE, GOING THROUGH VARIOUS GATES. AFTER A MILE (1.5 KM)
YOU PASS A RUINED BARN. CONTINUE THROUGH THE NEXT TWO GATES, THEN AS YOU
START TO ZIGZAG DOWN A SLOPE LOOK FOR A STANDING STONE BESIDE THE
TRACK. TURN SHARP LEFT HERE ONTO THE OLD LONDON TO HARLECH COACH ROAD.
(THE STONE HAS THE DISTANCES TO HARLECH AND TALYBONT CARVED ONTO ITS
SIDES.) 'COACH ROAD' IS A DECEPTIVELY GRAND TITLE FOR THIS NARROW TRACK. IT
MUST HAVE BEEN A SERIOUS CHALLENGE TO GET A STAGECOACH UP IT.

FOLLOW THE TRACK UP BESIDE THE WALL TO AN OLD IRON GATE WITH A WALLED GREEN
LANE BEYOND. RIDE UP THE LANE AND CONTINUE ALONG THE TRACK BEYOND. PASS
A GATE AND STILE (STANDING ON THEIR OWN - WITH NO FENCE OR WALL!) AND THEN GO
STRAIGHT ON ALONG A GRASSY PATH WHERE THE MORE OBVIOUS TRACK SWINGS
AWAY TO THE LEFT. CLIMB STEADILY UP THE SLOPE, FOLLOWING THE WALL ON
YOUR LEFT. AFTER PASSING THROUGH A COUPLE OF GATES YOU FIND YOURSELF WITH
A CLEAR STRETCH OF WALL HEADING STRAIGHT UP THE HILL IN FRONT OF YOU. CONTINUE
UPWARDS FOR 300 YARDS, BEARING LEFT TO A GATE. GO THROUGH AND CONTINUE
UPHILL TO A GRASSY PATH THAT ZIGZAGS UP THE SLOPE, THEN SWINGS AWAY TO

THE LEFT. CUTTING ACROSS THE HILLSIDE, IT CLIMBS STEADILY TO TAKE YOU TO THE TOP OF THE PASS.

WHEN YOU REACH THE TOP OF THE RIDGE YOU'RE GREETED BY A SUPERB VIEW - WITH MOUNTAINS ON YOUR RIGHT AND THE COAST STRETCHING AWAY TO THE LLEYN PENINSULA ON YOUR LEFT. IMMEDIATELY IN FRONT OF YOU THE TRACK DIPS AWAY OUT OF SIGHT - DOWNWARDS. A BIT OF GRAVITY ASSISTED TRAVEL IS WELL DESERVED AFTER SO MUCH CLIMBING, AND THE 800FT (250m) DROP OVER 1¼ MILES (2KM) IS UNLIKELY TO DISAPPOINT. WATCH OUT FOR ROCKY SECTIONS ON THE WAY DOWN, AND THE FINAL SECTION BEFORE THE BRIDGE CAN BE BOGGY (THERE'S A NARROW BOARDWALK WHICH WILL SERIOUSLY CHALLENGE YOUR SENSE OF BALANCE IF YOU TRY TO RIDE IT!).

THE OLD STONE BRIDGE AT PONT SCETHIN HAS AN AMAZING TIMELESS FEEL ABOUT IT, SITTING IN A BLEAK LANDSCAPE OF MOUNTAINS AND HILLS, UNSPOILT BY SIGNS OF MODERN LIFE. BEYOND THE BRIDGE FOLLOW THE TRACK, CLIMBING GENTLY FOR ½ MILE (0.75 KM) UNTIL YOU REACH A JUNCTION WITH ANOTHER TRACK. TURN LEFT ONTO WHAT BECOMES A SMOOTH, FAST 2 MILE (3KM) DESCENT (WITH A FEW GATES). WHEN YOU FINALLY REACH TARMAC TURN IMMEDIATELY LEFT, THROUGH ANOTHER GATE, AND FOLLOW THE LITTLE ROAD THROUGH AN AREA OF GORSEY SCRUBLAND. LOOK OUT FOR THE ROCKY REMAINS OF A PREHISTORIC BURIAL CHAMBER AMONGST THE BUSHES ON THE RIGHT OF THE ROAD. AFTER ½ MILE (0.75KM) YOU DROP DOWN, THROUGH A GATE, TO THE OLD STONE BRIDGE OF PONT FADOG. CONTINUE ALONG THE NARROW ROAD UNTIL IT ENDS AT ANOTHER GATE. THE GROUP OF OLD SCOTS PINES HERE WAS PROBABLY PLANTED AS A KIND OF EARLY INN SIGN - ADVERTISING A NEARBY RESTING PLACE FOR DROVERS CROSSING THE MOUNTAINS.

GO THROUGH THE GATE, TURNING RIGHT AND THEN GOING STRAIGHT ON WHERE THE TRACK FORKS AFTER A FEW YARDS. FOLLOW THE TRACK UP THROUGH A SERIES OF FIELDS (WHERE THE FARMER SEEMS TO BE GROWING AN IMPRESSIVE CROP OF ROCKS!). THE TRACK CLIMBS GENTLY IN A FAIRLY STRAIGHT LINE FOR 1½ MILES (2.5KM), HEADING TOWARDS A SMALL NOTCH ON THE SKYLINE. FOR THE FINAL 300FT (100m) OF HEIGHT GAIN THE TRACK STEEPENS TO BECOME A BOTTOM GEAR GRIND UP THE CRAGGY HILLSIDE.

AS YOU REACH THE TOP OF THE PASS A FANTASTIC VIEW SUDDENLY APPEARS IN FRONT OF YOU - ACROSS THE MAWDDACH ESTUARY TO THE DRAMATIC CLIFFS AND CRAGS OF CADAIR IDRIS. THIS IS A GREAT PLACE TO SIT AND REST, SOAK UP THE SCENERY AND BASK IN THE WARM GLOW THAT COMES FROM KNOWING THAT FROM HERE ITS DOWNHILL NEARLY ALL THE WAY BACK TO THE START - OVER 3 MILES (5KM) OF DESCENT! START THE DESCENT ON THE LITTLE PATH SWINGING AWAY TO THE LEFT DOWN THE HILL. WARP SPEED DOWNHILLERS BEWARE - THIS TRACK STARTS SMOOTH AND FAST BUT THERE ARE SOME VERY STEEP, SHARP HAIRPIN BENDS FURTHER DOWN. GO THROUGH A GATE HALFWAY DOWN AND DROP

Down through more zig zags until you reach a clear track just before a gate. Turn right, then right again onto another track. A short, gentle rise takes you to a gate and then you're onto a smooth fast 1 mile (1.5km) cruise, eventually taking you back onto tarmac by a farm. Take care on the narrow road descent as you zoom back down to the start.

THIS RIDE STARTS FROM THE VILLAGE OF LLANWDDYN (OR LLANWDDYN MARK 2 TO BE PRECISE - YOU'LL NEED A WETSUIT IF YOU WANT TO VISIT THE ORIGINAL VILLAGE!). THE NEW VILLAGE, DOMINATED BY VYRNWY LAKE AND DAM, WAS BUILT AT THE END OF THE 19TH CENTURY TO REPLACE THE VALLEY'S FLOODED COMMUNITIES.

THIS IS A FAIRLY EASY LITTLE ROUTE - IDEAL FOR BEGINNERS (OR ANYONE WHO FANCIES A RIDE THAT WON'T COMPLETELY SLAUGHTER THEM!)

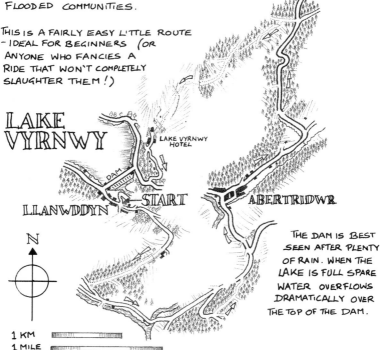

LAKE VYRNWY

LAKE VYRNWY HOTEL

DAM

LLANWDDYN · START · ABERTRIDWR

N

1 KM
1 MILE

THE DAM IS BEST SEEN AFTER PLENTY OF RAIN. WHEN THE LAKE IS FULL SPARE WATER OVERFLOWS DRAMATICALLY OVER THE TOP OF THE DAM.

ALTHOUGH SMALL, MODERN LLANWDDYN BOASTS CAFÉS AND A VISITOR CENTRE AND IS A POPULAR PLACE IN SUMMER. IF YOU VISIT WHEN IT'S BUSY TRY PARKING IN ONE OF THE CAR PARKS ALONG THE LAKE SHORE RATHER THAN IN THE OVERCROWDED VILLAGE.

THE 12 MILE (19 KM) ROAD CIRCUIT OF THE LAKE IS PLEASANT AND MOSTLY FLAT IF YOU FANCY EXTENDING THIS ROUTE.

Lake Vyrnwy

MAP: LANDRANGER 125 OR PATHFINDER 867 & 846
DISTANCE: 11 MILES / 17.5 KM   OFFROAD: 3½ MILES / 5.5 KM
TIME: 1-2 HOURS
HIGHEST POINT: 1450 FT / 440 M
TOTAL CLIMBING: 1400 FT / 430 M
START: LLANWDDYN   017 190

TAKE THE SMALL ROAD SOUTH EAST THROUGH THE VILLAGE AND
FOLLOW IT FOR ABOUT 1 MILE (1.5 KM), CLIMBING GENTLY UNTIL IT
BECOMES A TRACK BESIDE A FARM. THE TRACK CONTINUES TO
CLIMB FOR A LITTLE WAY THEN DROPS DOWN THROUGH A FOREST IN
A SUPERB SMOOTH 3/4 MILE (1KM) DESCENT. TURN LEFT AT THE
BOTTOM WHEN YOU MEET THE ROAD AND ROLL DOWN TO ANOTHER
JUNCTION. GO LEFT AGAIN AND RIDE DOWN THE VALLEY, CROSSING
THE AFON VYRNWY AND CLIMBING THE SHORT SLOPE BEYOND. IGNORE
THE RIGHT TURN AT THE TOP OF THE SLOPE BUT LOOK FOR
ANOTHER TURN 3/4 MILE (1KM) FURTHER ON. TURN RIGHT HERE
(TURNING BACK TO ALMOST FACE THE WAY YOU'VE JUST COME) AND
FOLLOW THE ROAD UP INTO THE WOOD. AFTER A LEFT BEND IGNORE
A TRACK OFF TO YOUR RIGHT BUT TAKE ANOTHER TRACK TO THE
LEFT A LITTLE FURTHER ON. THIS WELL SURFACED FOREST TRACK
CLIMBS FOR A COUPLE OF HUNDRED YARDS BEFORE DROPPING
BACK DOWN TO THE ROAD. TURN RIGHT ON THE ROAD AND THEN
SHORTLY, LEFT AT A T-JUNCTION AND ZOOM DOWN THE HILL
TO ABERTRIDWR.

TURN RIGHT IN THE VILLAGE - OPPOSITE THE TINY PETROL STATION.
FOLLOW THIS ROAD FOR 2 3/4 MILES (4.25 KM) CLIMBING GENTLY
UP THE VALLEY AND THROUGH A FOREST. IGNORE A RIGHT TURN
WHERE THE ROAD BENDS LEFT AFTER 1 MILE (1.5 KM) BUT LOOK
FOR ANOTHER SMALL ROAD ON THE RIGHT AS YOU REACH THE TOP
OF THE CLIMB. (IF YOU FIND YOURSELF ZOOMING DOWN A LONG FAST
DESCENT YOU'VE GONE TO FAR - TURN ROUND AND PEDAL BACK UP
AGAIN!) OPPOSITE THE RIGHT TURN - TURN LEFT ONTO A FOREST
TRACK. FOLLOW THE TRACK FOR A COUPLE OF HUNDRED YARDS AND
THEN TURN LEFT ONTO ANOTHER TRACK. FOLLOW THIS, PAST A PATH
OFF TO THE RIGHT AND THEN TURN UP A SECOND PATH ON THE RIGHT.
CLIMB UP THE PATH TO A T-JUNCTION, TURN RIGHT AND THEN LEFT
SHORTLY AFTERWARDS. BEAR LEFT AFTER ABOUT 100 YARDS
AND FOLLOW THE TRACK TO A GATE LEADING OUT ONTO OPEN
HILLSIDE.

THIS IS THE RIDE'S HIGHEST POINT AND IT'S NOW DOWNHILL ALL THE WAY BACK TO LLANWDDYN. BEYOND THE GATE STOP TO ADMIRE THE VIEWS OF THE LAKE AND MOUNTAINS BEYOND BEFORE DROPPING DOWN THE FIRST SECTION OF DESCENT TO ANOTHER GATE (WITH BILBERRIES GROWING ON THE GATE POST!). BEYOND THIS GATE THE TRACK GETS A BIT FAINT (ALTHOUGH BY THE TIME YOU RIDE THIS ROUTE THERE MAY BE SOME QUAD BIKE TRACKS TO ADD TO THE CONFUSION). HEAD DOWN THE FIELD, KEEPING THE FENCE IN SIGHT ON YOUR LEFT UNTIL YOU REACH A MORE DEFINED TRACK. FOLLOW THIS DOWN TO A GATE AT THE BOTTOM OF THE FIELD AND DROP DOWN PAST SOME STABLES TO THE LAKE VYRNWY HOTEL. FOLLOW THE LITTLE ROAD PAST THE BACK OF THE HOTEL, ROUND TO THE LEFT AND DOWN FOR ½ MILE (0.75 KM) TO A T-JUNCTION. TURN RIGHT AND THEN, AFTER A COUPLE OF HUNDRED YARDS, LEFT ACROSS THE DAM BACK TO LLANWDDYN.

THINGS TO SEE — RESERVOIRS

ONE OF THE MOST DRAMATIC WAYS THAT PEOPLE ALTER THE LANDSCAPE IS BY CREATING RESERVOIRS. TODAY WE TAKE OUR WATER SUPPLY FOR GRANTED, BUT THINGS HAVEN'T ALWAYS BEEN THIS WAY. IN THE LATE 19th CENTURY POOR WATER SUPPLIES WERE CAUSING MAJOR OUTBREAKS OF TYPHOID AND OTHER DISEASES IN LARGE TOWNS AND CITIES. THE FIRST MAJOR RESERVOIR PROJECT IN WALES WAS LAKE VYRNWY IN THE 1880'S. THEN THE LARGEST RESERVOIR IN EUROPE, IT PROVIDED CLEAN, FRESH WATER TO LIVERPOOL. THE FIRST DAMS AT ELAN WERE BUILT SHORTLY AFTER TO SUPPLY WATER TO BIRMINGHAM.

THE DAMS WERE MAJOR FEATS OF ENGINEERING. TEMPORARY VILLAGES WERE BUILT FOR THE THOUSANDS OF WORKERS AND RAILWAYS WERE USED TO TRANSPORT MATERIALS (33 MILES OF TRACK WERE LAID IN THE ELAN VALLEYS!). NEW HOMES ALSO HAD TO BE BUILT TO REPLACE THE FLOODED FARMS AND VILLAGES. MANY RESERVOIRS HAD FORESTS PLANTED AROUND THEM. THE TREES PREVENTED ANIMALS AND SOIL EROSION FROM POLLUTING THE WATER, AND FORESTRY PROVIDED NEW JOBS FOR LOCAL PEOPLE.

TODAY THERE ARE NUMEROUS RESERVOIRS IN MID-WALES, PROVIDING WATER, AND SOME ALSO PRODUCING HYDRO-ELECTRICITY. WHILST A FLOODED VALLEY IS NOT IDEAL FOR MOUNTAIN BIKING, RECREATIONAL ACCESS IS OFTEN ENCOURAGED IN THE SURROUNDING COUNTRYSIDE.

ALTHOUGH MAN-MADE, MANY RESERVOIRS ARE ATTRACTIVE LANDSCAPE FEATURES AND HAVENS FOR WILDLIFE.

HERON

LOOK OUT DURING DROUGHTS WHEN WATER LEVELS DROP REVEALING THE REMAINS OF OLD ROADS AND BUILDINGS.

DON'T CAUSE POLLUTION IN RESERVOIRS OR SURROUNDING STREAMS — IT MIGHT BE YOUR OWN DRINKING WATER!

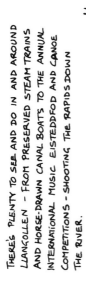

THERE'S PLENTY TO SEE AND DO IN AND AROUND
LLANGOLLEN - FROM PRESERVED STEAM TRAINS
AND HORSE-DRAWN CANAL BOATS TO THE ANNUAL
INTERNATIONAL MUSIC EISTEDDFOD AND CANOE
COMPETITIONS - SHOOTING THE RAPIDS DOWN
THE RIVER.

THERE'S PLENTY OF SCENERY TOO - THE
RIVER DEE IN ITS DEEP TWISTING VALLEY,
THE DRAMATIC RUINS OF CASTELL DINAS
BRAN, HUGE LIMESTONE CLIFFS STRETCHING
UP THE VALLEY TO WORLD'S END AND THE
HIGH, RUGGED HILLS BEYOND.

FOR A MOUNTAIN BIKE RIDE THIS
ROUTE INVOLVES A LOT OF ROAD RIDING
- BUT THESE ARE PRETTY MOUNTAINOUS
ROADS. THE CLIMBS PAST CASTELL
DINAS BRAN AND UP TO WORLD'S END
ARE REAL LUNG BURSTERS AND
THE DESCENT OF THE
HORSESHOE PASS IS
TRULY AWESOME. THERE'S
ALSO ENOUGH OFFROAD
SECTIONS THROWN IN TO
MAKE SURE YOU GO HOME MUDDY!

WORLD'S END

CYRN-Y-BRAIN

HORSESHOE PASS

OLD QUARRY

MOEL Y FAEN

MOEL Y GAMELIN

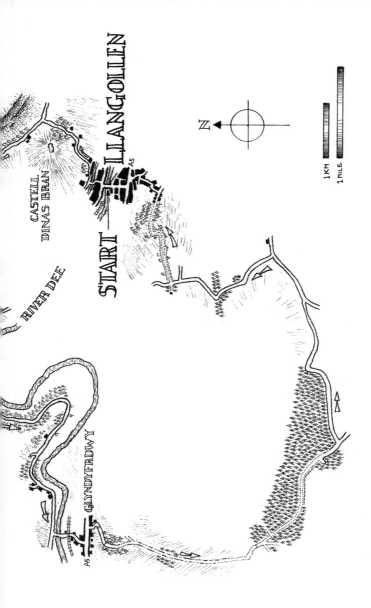

41

HORSESHOE PASS

MAP: LANDRANGERS 116, 117, 125 (PLUS A VERY SMALL BIT OF 126). PATHFINDERS 789, 805, 806, 826 (827)

DISTANCE: 33 MILES / 53 KM   OFFROAD: 6 MILES / 9.5 KM

TIME: 3-6 HOURS

HIGHEST POINT: 1575 FT / 480 M

TOTAL CLIMBING: 3650 FT / 1110 M

START: LLANGOLLEN   215 421

START ON THE BRIDGE IN THE CENTRE OF LLANGOLLEN. AT THE T-JUNCTION AT THE END OF THE BRIDGE TURN RIGHT AND THEN IMMEDIATELY LEFT (BY THE TAXIDERMIST'S SHOP!). CLIMB UP THE STEEP ROAD, OVER THE CANAL BRIDGE AND TURN RIGHT. THIS LITTLE ROAD TAKES YOU UP PAST THE STEEP SIDED HILL CROWNED WITH THE RUINS OF CASTELL DINAS BRAN, TO THE DRAMATIC LIMESTONE CLIFFS OF TREVOR ROCKS. AT THE TOP TURN LEFT AND FOLLOW THE ROAD UP THE VALLEY WITH THE CLIFFS TOWERING ABOVE YOU ON YOUR RIGHT. 4 MILES (6.5 KM) OF GENTLE TARMAC BRING YOU TO THE HEAD OF THE VALLEY AT WORLD'S END! SPLASH THROUGH THE FORD AND GRIND UP THE STEEP ROAD UP TO THE EDGE OF THE OPEN MOOR.

CONTINUE UP THE ROAD FOR ANOTHER 3/4 MILE (1KM) THEN TURN LEFT ONTO A TRACK BY A SIGN FOR THE OFFA'S DYKE PATH. PART OF THIS TRACK IS ON NARROW BOARDWALKS WHICH REQUIRE A BIT OF CONCENTRATION AND BALANCE - ESPECIALLY WHEN THEY'RE WET. (KEEP TO THE BOARDWALKS TO ALLOW THE ERODED SECTIONS OF PATH TO HEAL.) WHEN YOU REACH THE EDGE OF THE FOREST GO STRAIGHT ON, THROUGH THE DOUBLE GATE. MUD, RUTS AND ROOTS LEAD YOU TO A LARGE GRAVEL FOREST ROAD. GO STRAIGHT ACROSS AND HEAD DOWN THE START OF A BRILLIANT 1¼ MILE (2KM) DESCENT. (PARTS OF THIS TRACK CAN GET VERY MUDDY IN WINTER.) CROSS ANOTHER BIG TRACK AND TAKE THE LEFT ONE OF THE TWO DESCENDING TRACKS. WHEN YOU REACH A SMALL ARTIFICIAL STREAM, CROSS THE PLANK BRIDGE, SWING LEFT ALONG THE BANK AND THEN TURN RIGHT DOWN THE SLOPE AGAIN. A SHARP RIGHT, THEN LEFT AT THE NEXT JUNCTION

TAKES YOU DOWN A STEEP, ROCKY DIP TO SOME MUDDY PUDDLES. THEN THE PATH BECOMES SMOOTH AND FAST, CROSSES ANOTHER BIG TRACK AND TAKES YOU FINALLY DOWN TO A GATE. TAKE IT GENTLY DOWN THE NARROW PATH BEYOND THE GATE, PAST A HIDDEN HOUSE ENTRANCE, TO THE ROAD. TURN LEFT AND CLIMB GENTLY ALONG THE GATED ROAD UNTIL YOU EVENTUALLY MEET A MAIN ROAD. TURN LEFT AND CLIMB STEADILY FOR 1¼ MILES (2 KM) UNTIL YOU REACH THE REWARDING SIGHT OF THE CAFÉ AT THE TOP OF THE PASS.

CONTINUE PAST THE CAFÉ. AS THE VIEW OPENS UP INFRONT OF YOU THE ROAD STARTS TO GENTLY DESCEND DOWN THE FAR SIDE OF THE PASS. THIS IS A TRULY AWESOME DESCENT - EVEN IF IT IS ALL ON TARMAC. YOU CAN HIT SOME SERIOUS SPEED DOWN HERE - BUT WATCH OUT FOR CATTLE GRIDS, SHARP BENDS, STUPID SHEEP AND EVEN STUPIDER DRIVERS. AFTER 3 MILES (5 KM) OF WARP SPEED PLUMMET, TURN RIGHT ONTO A SMALL ROAD (400 YARDS AFTER PASSING THE BRITANNIA INN ON YOUR RIGHT). FOLLOW THIS ROAD UNTIL IT TAKES YOU TO A T-JUNCTION. TURN RIGHT AND FOLLOW THE LITTLE ROAD ON A SCENIC CRUISE UP THE DEE VALLEY FOR 4½ MILES (7 KM). EVENTUALLY YOU TURN LEFT, ACROSS A BRIDGE TOWARDS GLYNDYFRDWY.

GLYNDYFRDWY MAY SEEM LIKE A FAIRLY UNREMARKABLE VILLAGE, BUT IT HOLDS A UNIQUE PLACE IN WELSH HISTORY. IT WAS NEAR HERE IN 1400 THAT OWAIN GLYNDŴR WAS CROWNED PRINCE OF WALES BY HIS SUPPORTERS, AT THE START OF HIS GREAT REBELLION AGAINST THE ENGLISH.

CROSS THE LEVEL CROSSING OVER THE TRACKS OF THE LLANGOLLEN STEAM RAILWAY. (TRAINS RUN MOST DAYS DURING THE SUMMER AND MOST WEEKENDS FOR THE REST OF THE YEAR.) CONTINUE ALONG THE ROAD UP TO THE T-JUNCTION IN GLYNDYFRDWY VILLAGE. TURN LEFT ONTO THE BUSY A5 AND AFTER 250 YARDS TURN RIGHT JUST PAST THE CHURCH AND GO UP A SMALL ROAD SIGNED AS 'UNSUITABLE FOR MOTORS'. PASS A COUPLE OF HOUSES AND GO THROUGH A GATE. BY A SECOND GATE YOU CAN SEE THE RUINED WINDING HOUSE OF AN OLD TRAMWAY INCLINE, WHERE SLATE FROM NEARBY QUARRIES WAS TAKEN DOWN TO THE RAILWAY. CONTINUE UP THE DERELICT ROAD ON A LONG, STEADY CLIMB THROUGH A WOOD AND UP THE VALLEY SIDE. MOST OF THIS OLD ROAD CAN REALLY BE COUNTED AS OFFROAD - WITH PLENTY OF PLACES WHERE THE TARMAC HAS COMPLETELY DISAPPEARED. EVENTUALLY YOU REACH LEVEL GROUND ON THE HILLTOP AND ENTER THE CEIRIOG FOREST. BEAR LEFT AT A JUNCTION AND CONTINUE ALONG THE TRACK/ROAD WHICH BECOMES FAST AS IT GENTLY DESCENDS. PAST A FOREST CAR PARK THE TARMAC BECOMES MORE OBVIOUS AND TURNS INTO A PROPER ROAD.

AT A JUNCTION AT THE EDGE OF THE FOREST TURN LEFT. GO STRAIGHT ON AFTER 2 MILES (3·5 KM) THEN LEFT AFTER ANOTHER MILE (1·5 KM). AFTER A FURTHER 1½ MILES (2·5 KM) TURN RIGHT ONTO A BRIDLEWAY OPPOSITE A TRACK TO A FARM CALLED FFYNNON LAS. THIS IS AN EXCELLENT GREEN LANE DESCENT, DROPPING BACK DOWN INTO LLANGOLLEN. YOU EMERGE ONTO TARMAC BY SOME HOUSES AND AFTER 300 YARDS TURN LEFT, DOWN PAST THE CEMETARY. AT THE T-JUNCTION TURN RIGHT AND THEN LEFT TO TAKE YOU DOWN TO THE A5. TURN LEFT TO THE TRAFFIC LIGHTS AND THEN RIGHT DOWN THE MAIN STREET BACK TO THE START.

▼ Approaching Worlds End!

THINGS TO SEE ~ LEGENDARY HEROES

THE CELTIC SPIRIT SEEMS TO INSPIRE HEROES. IT ALSO SEEMS TO INSPIRE STORYTELLERS. THROUGHOUT WALES AND THE MARCHES YOU'LL COME ACROSS A WEALTH OF FANTASTIC TALES ABOUT HEROIC MEN AND WOMEN. SOME ARE OBVIOUSLY FICTIONAL, BUT OTHERS WERE REAL HISTORICAL CHARACTERS.

CARACTACUS

WAS A WARRIOR CHIEFTAIN IN SOUTH-EAST BRITAIN AT THE TIME OF THE ROMAN INVASION. HE FLED WEST AND RALLIED THE WELSH TRIBES TO A FINAL STAND AGAINST THE INVADERS. UNFORTUNATELY THE BRITISH WERE NO MATCH FOR THE INVINCIBLE MIGHT OF THE ROMAN ARMY. AFTER THEIR DEFEAT CARACTACUS AGAIN FLED, BUT THE QUEEN OF A RIVAL TRIBE BETRAYED HIM AND HE WAS CAPTURED AND TAKEN TO ROME IN CHAINS, AS A WAR TROPHY. THERE HE MANAGED TO IMPRESS THE EMPEROR SO MUCH THAT INSTEAD OF BEING EXECUTED HE WAS RELEASED. BUT INSTEAD OF RETURNING TO HIS TRIBE, HE DECIDED THE ROMAN WAY OF LIFE SUITED HIM AND HE SPENT THE REST OF HIS DAYS LIVING IN A LUXURY VILLA IN ROME.

LLYWELYN THE GREAT

WAS THE GREATEST LORD IN MEDIEVAL WALES. HE BROUGHT THE OTHER WELSH LORDS TOGETHER UNDER HIS POWER - EFFECTIVELY CREATING A UNIFIED WALES, CAPABLE OF RESISTING THE LORDS OF THE MARCHES WHO HAD BEEN SEIZING WELSH LAND. THE ENGLISH KING WAS UNIMPRESSED AND LAUNCHED ATTACKS ON WALES, BUT WITH LIMITED SUCCESS. LLYWELYN RECAPTURED MOST OF THE LOST WELSH TERRITORY AND ALSO EXPANDED EAST INTO THE MARCHES. UNFORTUNATELY IT DIDN'T LAST. AFTER HIS DEATH HIS SONS WERE TOO BUSY FIGHTING EACH OTHER TO FIGHT THE ENGLISH, AND ALTHOUGH HIS GRANDSON - LLYWELYN THE LAST - BECAME AS POWERFUL AS 'L THE G', HE PUSHED HIS LUCK TOO FAR AND PROVOKED THE ENGLISH INVASION AND CONQUEST OF WALES.

OWAIN GLYNDŴR.

A HUNDRED YEARS AFTER THE CONQUEST OF WALES THERE WAS STILL DEEP RESENTMENT AGAINST ENGLISH RULE. IN 1400 GLYNDŴR'S SUPPORTERS CROWNED HIM PRINCE OF WALES (AT GLYNDYFRDWY NEAR LLANGOLLEN). BY 1404 HE HAD CAPTURED HARLECH AND ABERYSTWYTH CASTLES AND ESTABLISHED A PARLIAMENT AT MACHYNLLETH WITH POWERS OVER MUCH OF WALES. EVENTUALLY THE ENGLISH REGAINED CONTROL, BUT OWAIN GLYNDŴR SIMPLY VANISHED INTO THE HILLS AND WAS NEVER CAPTURED.

CADAIR IDRIS (MEANING 'THE CHAIR OF IDRIS'- A LEGENDARY GIANT) IS ONE OF
SNOWDONIA'S MOST DRAMATIC MOUNTAINS. AT 2930 FT (893m) ITS
A SERIOUS CLIMB - ESPECIALLY AS THE START IS ONLY 80FT (25m)
ABOVE SEA LEVEL. THIS ROUTE SHOULD BE TREATED AS A
MOUNTAINEERING EXPEDITION - INVOLVING ROUGH AND EXPOSED
TERRAIN WITH LONG STRETCHES WHERE YOU HAVE NO CHOICE BUT TO CARRY
YOUR BIKE. THE REWARDS FOR YOUR EFFORTS ARE FANTASTIC SCENERY
AND BRILLIANT VIEWS, THE INDEFINABLE
SENSE OF SATISFACTION FROM
CONQUERING HIGH ALTITUDES
AND, OF COURSE, THE
6 MILE (9KM) DESCENT!

LLYN Y GADAIR

CADAIR IDRIS

2930FT
893M

LLYN CAU

FOR POST-RIDE CHILL OUT TRY
EXPLORING THE GNARLED OLD RUINS
OF CASTELL Y BERE - A BRILLIANT
PLACE TO SPEND THE END OF AN
AFTERNOON, RELAXING AND SOAKING
UP THE ATMOSPHERE OF THIS BEAUTIFUL
CORNER OF WALES.

N

CASTELL Y BERE
LLANFIHANGEL
-Y-PENNANT
START
CAR
PARK

1 KM
1 MILE

DOLGELLAU
A493
LLANFIHANGEL
-Y-PENNANT
ABERGYNOLWYN
A487
TYWYN
A493
MACHYNLLETH

46

Cadair Idris

MAP: LANDRANGER 124 OR OUTDOOR LEISURE 23
DISTANCE: 12 MILES / 19 KM   OFFROAD: 10½ MILES / 17 KM
TIME: 3-6½ HOURS
HIGHEST POINT: 2930 FT / 893 M
TOTAL CLIMBING: 2850 FT / 870 M
START: LLANFIHANGEL-Y-PENNANT   672 088   CAR PARK OPPOSITE CHAPEL

SOME SPECIAL BITS OF KIT AND PREPARATION ARE RECOMMENDED FOR THIS RIDE.
SPARE CLOTHES – IT'S ALWAYS COLDER AT THE SUMMIT THAN IT IS AT THE
BOTTOM. EVEN IN SUMMER YOU'LL NEED TO CARRY TROUSERS, A WINDPROOF TOP AND
A GOOD WATERPROOF.
FOOTWEAR – THIS ROUTE INCLUDES LONG SECTIONS OF WALKING ON VERY
ROUGH TRACKS. LIGHTWEIGHT WALKING BOOTS ARE BEST - WITH FLAT PEDALS WITH
OR WITHOUT TOECLIPS AND STRAPS.
FOOD & DRINK – TAKE LOADS OF HIGH ENERGY FUEL. – YOU'LL NEED IT!
PADDING – YOU'LL BE DOING A LOT OF CARRYING - SO
ITS A GOOD IDEA TO WORK OUT THE BEST WAY TO DO IT.
FOR MOST NORMAL BIKES - PUT YOUR ARM THROUGH
THE MAIN FRAME TRIANGLE AND GRAB THE
HANDLEBARS, WITH THE TOP TUBE / SEAT TUBE
JOIN RESTING ON YOUR SHOULDER. STRAPPING A BIT OF PADDING TO THE FRAME
WHERE IT RESTS ON YOUR SHOULDER WILL SAVE YOU A LOT OF DISCOMFORT.
WHEN TO GO – THE BEST TIMES ARE LATE SPRING / EARLY SUMMER OR
LATE SUMMER / EARLY AUTUMN. AVOID WEEKENDS IN MIDSUMMER (UNLESS YOU
WANT TO QUEUE UP TO REACH THE SUMMIT!) AND DON'T EVEN THINK ABOUT
IT IN WINTER (IF YOU MUST GO UP THEN - LEAVE YOUR BIKE BEHIND AND TAKE CRAMPONS
AND AN ICE AXE INSTEAD!). GET A DETAILED WEATHER FORECAST WHENEVER YOU GO.
(MOUNTAINCALL SNOWDONIA - 0891 500 449). IF ITS BAD - DON'T GO.

HEAD UP THE VALLEY ON THE LITTLE ROAD. THE FIRST 3/4 MILE (1 KM) IS
DECEPTIVELY FLAT. OVER A BRIDGE THE ROAD SWINGS RIGHT ALONGSIDE THE
RIVER, THEN AS THE TARMAC FADES AWAY THE CLIMBING BEGINS. FROM HERE
IT'S UPHILL ALL THE WAY TO THE SUMMIT. AFTER A COUPLE OF MINUTES CLIMBING
YOU PASS THROUGH A DOUBLE SET OF GATES AND THEN TURN RIGHT OFF THE MAIN
TRACK ONTO A PATH BESIDE A WALL. FOLLOW THIS TO A PRETTY LITTLE STREAM
WITH A STONE SLAB FOOTBRIDGE. THE PATH BEYOND THE STREAM IS STEEP AND
YOU'LL BE WALKING BY THE TIME YOU REACH A GATE. THROUGH THE GATE CONTINUE
TO A WALL AND FOLLOW IT UP THE GENTLE SLOPE. EVENTUALLY THE FAINT PATH
SWINGS AWAY FROM THE WALL THROUGH A PATCH OF REEDS TO THE BIG SMOOTH TRACK.
TURN RIGHT AND RIDE TO A GATE.

BEYOND THE GATE IT'S ½ MILE (0.8 KM) OF SMOOTH, GENTLE CLIMBING.
THE TRACK SWINGS TO THE LEFT INTO A BIG SIDE VALLEY. GO THROUGH A
GATE AND THEN FURTHER ON, WHERE THE MAIN TRACK SWINGS UP TO THE
LEFT, BEAR RIGHT TO ANOTHER GATE. THROUGH THE GATE THE TRACK
TAKES YOU TO A FORD AND THEN ZIGZAGS STEEPLY UP THE HILL BEYOND.
SHORTLY AFTER PASSING THROUGH A GATE THE GRADIENT EASES FOR A
(RELATIVELY) ENJOYABLE 1¼ MILE (2KM) OF GENTLE SINGLETRACK CLIMBING.
YOU EVENTUALLY REACH A GATE ON TOP OF THE RIDGE WITH BRILLIANT
VIEWS TO THE NORTH SUDDENLY REVEALED BEFORE YOU.

FROM HERE THE CHARACTER OF THE RIDE CHANGES DRAMATICALLY. THE
HILLSIDE IS LITTERED WITH JAGGED ROCKS AND THE TRACK BECOMES A
REAL CHALLENGE. RIDING IS IMPOSSIBLE IN MANY PLACES AND EVEN WALKING
CAN BE TRICKY ON THE UNEVEN SURFACE (ESPECIALLY WITH A CUMBERSOME
PIECE OF TWO WHEELED LUGGAGE SLUNG OVER YOUR SHOULDER!). IT ALSO

48

GETS QUITE BUSY WITH WALKERS. AFTER 1 MILE (1.5 KM) OF MOSTLY PUSHING OR CARRYING YOU EMERGE ONTO FLAT GROUND NEAR THE SUMMIT. BEWARE — AHEAD AND TO YOUR LEFT TRULY AWE INSPIRING (AND VERTIGO INDUCING!) CLIFFS PLUNGE 800FT (250m) TO THE WATERS OF LLYN Y CADAIR FAR BELOW. THE FINAL SCRAMBLE TO THE SUMMIT IS A TRICKY BIT OF CARRYING — TAKE IT SLOWLY AND MAKE SURE YOU HAVE ONE HAND FREE TO GRAB HOLD OF ROCKS.

THE SUMMIT AREA IS A JUMBLED PILE OF ROCKS AND CRAGS DROPPING AWAY DOWN AWESOME CLIFFS ON TWO SIDES AND WITH TRULY BREATHTAKING VIEWS.

AFTER ALL THE EFFORT INVOLVED GETTING UP HERE IT SEEMS A PITY TO HAVE TO LEAVE — BUT EVENTUALLY YOU HAVE TO TEAR YOURSELF AWAY AND START THE DESCENT. BACK DOWN THE WAY YOU CAME UP — BUT THIS TIME WITH GRAVITY ON YOUR SIDE. THE SCRAMBLE, CARRYING YOUR BIKE, DOWN FROM THE SUMMIT IS JUST AS TRICKY GOING DOWN AS IT WAS GOING UP. AFTER A COUPLE OF HUNDRED YARDS THOUGH, YOU CAN ENJOY THE NOVELTY OF PUTTING YOUR WHEELS BACK ON THE GROUND. THE FIRST MILE (1.5 KM) OF DESCENT IS SERIOUSLY GNARLY. YOU'RE UNLIKELY TO BE ABLE TO RIDE IT ALL — SO IF IN DOUBT, GET OFF AND WALK. THIS IS NO PLACE TO RISK BREAKING YOUR BODY OR BIKE. GIVE WAY TO WALKERS AND BE EXTRA CAREFUL TO AVOID EROSION — ESPECIALLY ON LOOSE SECTIONS. (DON'T RIP UP THE TRACK UNLESS YOU'RE PREPARED TO PUSH A WHEELBARROW FULL OF ROCKS UP HERE TO MEND IT!)

EVENTUALLY YOU REACH THE GATE, BEYOND WHICH YOU RETURN TO SMOOTH GRASSY SINGLETRACK. THE REST OF THE DESCENT IS LIKE ALL YOUR FAVOURITE DOWNHILLS STUCK TOGETHER. SMOOTH BITS, FAST BITS, NARROW BITS AND STEEP BITS. PLUS A SMATTERING OF ROCKS AND BUMPS TO KEEP YOU ON YOUR TOES ALL THE WAY BACK DOWN TO THE LITTLE ROAD IN THE VALLEY.

▼ The summit cairn

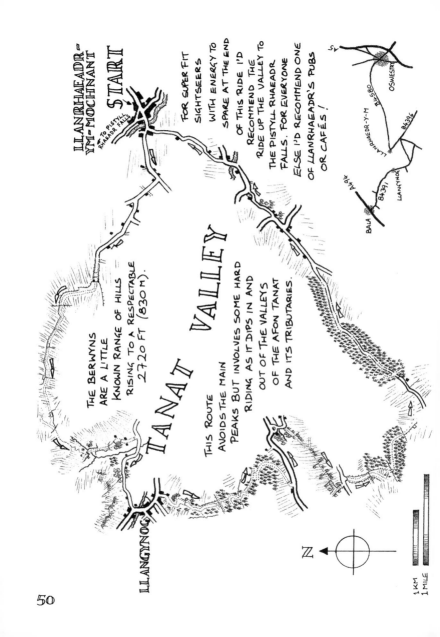

LLANRHAEADR-YM-MOCHNANT **START**

TO PISTYLL RHAEADR FALLS

FOR SUPER FIT SIGHTSEERS WITH ENERGY TO SPARE AT THE END OF THIS RIDE I'D RECOMMEND THE RIDE UP THE VALLEY TO THE PISTYLL RHAEADR FALLS. FOR EVERYONE ELSE I'D RECOMMEND ONE OF LLANRHAEADR'S PUBS OR CAFÉS!

THE BERWYNS ARE A LITTLE KNOWN RANGE OF HILLS RISING TO A RESPECTABLE 2720 FT (830 M).

TANAT VALLEY

THIS ROUTE AVOIDS THE MAIN PEAKS BUT INVOLVES SOME HARD RIDING AS IT DIPS IN AND OUT OF THE VALLEYS OF THE AFON TANAT AND ITS TRIBUTARIES.

LLANGYNOG

N

1 KM
1 MILE

OSWESTRY

B4580

LLANRHAEADR-Y-M

B4396

A495

A490

B4391

BALA

LLANGYNOG

TANAT VALLEY & THE BERWYNS ROUTE 7

MAP: LANDRANGER 125 OR PATHFINDER 846
DISTANCE: 18½ MILES / 29.5 KM   OFFROAD: 9 MILES / 14.5 KM
TIME: 2½ – 4 HOURS
HIGHEST POINT: 1700 FT / 518 M
TOTAL CLIMBING: 3300 FT / 1000 M
START: LLANRHAEADR-YM-MOCHNANT 124 261 (OR LLANGYNOG 053 262)

FOLLOW THE ROAD WEST OUT OF THE VILLAGE (TOWARDS PENYBONTFAWR).
AFTER 3/4 MILE (1 KM) TURN RIGHT AT THE TOP OF THE HILL. FORK LEFT
AFTER ½ MILE (0.75 KM) AND THEN GO STRAIGHT ON WHERE THE ROAD
BENDS ROUND TO THE LEFT A FEW HUNDRED YARDS FURTHER ON. THIS LANE
CLIMBS GENTLY FOR 1 MILE (1.5 KM) TURNING INTO A TRACK SHORTLY BEFORE
REACHING A BARN. GO THROUGH THE GATE BY THE BARN AND FOLLOW THE
TRACK ROUND TO THE RIGHT OF THE HILLSIDE. THIS IS A GOOD, CLEAR TRACK
WITH OCCASIONAL GATES AND FANTASTIC VIEWS UP THE RHAEADR VALLEY
TO THE PISTYLL RHAEADR WATERFALL. FOLLOW THE TRACK FOR 2 MILES
(3 KM) TO A SHEEP PEN IN A BOG (NOT THE FIRST SHEEP PEN YOU PASS).
BEYOND THE SHEEP PEN THE GROUND IS BOGGY (BEST WALKED) AND THE TRACK
VIRTUALLY DISAPPEARS. GO STRAIGHT ON - FOLLOWING THE FENCE ON YOUR
LEFT - UNTIL YOU REACH A CLEARER TRACK AFTER 100 YARDS OR SO.

TURN LEFT ON THE TRACK TO A GATE AND STILE. BEYOND THE GATE THE
PATH IS FAIRLY FAINT AND NARROW. FOLLOW IT ACROSS THE HILL
AND DROP DOWN INTO THE VALLEY ON THE FAR SIDE. THIS DESCENT
IS SCARY STEEP - WITH A FEW SLIGHT ZIG ZAGS BUT MOSTLY HEADING
STRAIGHT DOWN. TAKE IT EASY IN THE WET AND WATCH OUT FOR THE
MINE TUNNEL ENTRANCE NEAR THE BOTTOM. (JUST TO THE RIGHT OF
THE PATH - YOU CAN'T SEE IT UNTIL YOU'RE ALMOST OVER IT!) GO THROUGH
A GATE AT THE BOTTOM AND FOLLOW THE OBVIOUS TRACK DOWN THROUGH
A FEW MORE GATES AND PAST A COUPLE OF FARMS TO THE ROAD.

HIT THE ROAD AND TURN RIGHT FOR A MILE (1.5 KM) TO A T-JUNCTION.
TURN LEFT AND FOLLOW THE ROAD OVER A BRIDGE AND THROUGH LLANGYNOG.
(STOP AT THE PUBS OR CAFÉS IF YOU FANCY A BREAK.) OVER ANOTHER BRIDGE
AND THEN, AFTER PASSING A ROAD ON THE RIGHT, TURN RIGHT UP A TRACK
(BRIDLEWAY SIGN AT JUNCTION). PASS A COUPLE OF BUNGALOWS AND
CONTINUE TO SOME OLD QUARRY WORKINGS. IT'S WORTH STOPPING TO ADMIRE
THE SUPERB VIEWS. ACROSS THE VALLEY YOU CAN SEE THE OLD INCLINE
FROM LLANGYNOG UP TO THE HILLTOP SLATE MINES WHERE HARD MEN
ONCE SPENT HARD LIVES QUARRYING THE CRAGS AND CLIFFS. YOUR OWN
HARD LIFE CONTINUES WITH A CLIMB UP THROUGH OLD SPOIL TIPS AND

PAST A COTTAGE. FOLLOW THE TRACK UP THE EDGE OF A YOUNG FOREST PLANTATION, IGNORING TRACKS OFF TO THE SIDE, UNTIL YOU REACH THE EDGE OF A MATURE FOREST. GO STRAIGHT INTO THE FOREST FOR APPROX 100 YARDS THEN LEFT ON THE MAIN TRACK. AFTER ANOTHER COUPLE OF HUNDRED YARDS LOOK FOR A SMALL TRACK OFF TO YOUR LEFT (SIGNPOSTED AS A BRIDLEWAY). FOLLOW THIS TRACK FOR ABOUT ½ MILE (¾ KM) UNTIL IT MEETS A LARGE FOREST TRACK WHICH GIVES A FAST DESCENT DOWN TO THE ROAD.

TURN LEFT ON THE ROAD, THEN RIGHT AFTER ¾ MILE (1KM) DOWN A SMALL ROAD WHICH CROSSES A STREAM AND CLIMBS FOR ABOUT 200 YARDS TO A LEFT BEND. TURN RIGHT HERE ONTO A BRIDLEWAY AND FOLLOW IT THROUGH A GATE AND OUT ACROSS A STEEP HILLSIDE FIELD. WHERE THE TRACK DOUBLES BACK TO YOUR LEFT CONTINUE STRAIGHT AHEAD CLIMBING ACROSS THE HILLSIDE ON A FAINT PATH. GO THROUGH A GATE AT THE FAR SIDE OF THE FIELD AND FOLLOW THE TRACK UNTIL IT EVENTUALLY MEETS ANOTHER AT A T-JUNCTION. GO LEFT AND DROP DOWN THE NARROW HEDGED PATH TO THE ROAD. CROSS THE ROAD ONTO A BIG WIDE TRACK WHICH CLIMBS GENTLY THROUGH FIELDS TO THE EDGE OF A FOREST. CONTINUE UP THE TRACK, WITH TREES ON YOUR LEFT UNTIL YOU SEE A SMALL SIGNPOSTED PATH ON YOUR LEFT. DROP DOWN THIS PATH, ALONG THE FOREST EDGE TO A LITTLE BRIDGE AND GATE AND THEN FOLLOW IT UP THROUGH THE FOREST TO YOUR LEFT. THIS ANCIENT TRACKWAY - THE LLWYBR HEULEN - EVENTUALLY EMERGES FROM THE FOREST BY A GATE INTO A FIELD. GO STRAIGHT AHEAD, FOLLOWING THE FENCE ON YOUR RIGHT UNTIL, AFTER PASSING A SHEEP PEN, YOU SWING LEFT ON WHAT LOOKS SUSPICIOUSLY LIKE A SHEEP TRACK - BUT IS ACTUALLY A BRIDLEWAY. THIS SWOOPS ACROSS THE HILLSIDE TO MEET A LITTLE ROAD.

IN THEORY IT'S NOW TARMAC ALL THE WAY BACK TO LLAN RHAEADR-Y-M. IN REALITY YOU'LL FIND THERE'S STILL SOME ROUGH STUFF TO COME. FOLLOW THE ROAD TO A GATE INTO A FOREST. THE ROAD DOWN THROUGH THE WOOD IS A 2 MILE (3KM) DESCENT OF MUD, GRAVEL, POTHOLES AND PUDDLES (THERE IS SOME TARMAC - BUT YOU'LL HAVE TO LOOK QUITE HARD TO FIND IT!). WATCH OUT FOR THE JUNCTION AT THE BOTTOM - NO SIGNS OR OTHER WARNINGS - AND YOU'RE LIKELY TO BE APPROACHING FAST. GO STRAIGHT ON DOWN TO THE B-ROAD AND THEN TURN LEFT. TURN RIGHT ONTO ANOTHER SMALL ROAD AFTER 200 YARDS - WHERE THE MAIN ROAD BENDS LEFT. AT THE NEXT T-JUNCTION GO RIGHT, THEN SHORTLY AFTER CROSSING THE AFON TANAT TURN LEFT (EFFECTIVELY STRAIGHT ON) WHERE THE ROAD BENDS ROUND TO THE RIGHT. THE FINAL MILE OF ROAD CLIMBS OVER A LITTLE HILL AND DROPS STEEPLY BACK DOWN INTO LLAN RHAEADR - YM- MOCHNANT.

Looking up the valley towards Pistyll Rhaeadr and the Berwyns ▶

THINGS TO SEE — WELSH PLACE NAMES

EVEN MOST WELSH PEOPLE ADMIT THE WELSH LANGUAGE ISN'T EASY . FOR ENGLISH
SPEAKERS IT CAN BE A REAL TONGUE TWISTER . WELSH IS A CELTIC LANGUAGE
SIMILAR TO GAELIC , CORNISH AND BRETON (THE LANGUAGE OF ASTERIX THE GAUL!).
ITS TOTALLY DIFFERENT FROM ENGLISH WHICH IS DERIVED FROM ELEMENTS OF
LATIN , GERMAN , FRENCH AND DUTCH (AMONGST OTHERS!).

JUST TO CONFUSE THINGS YOU'LL NOTICE CERTAIN LETTERS ARE OFTEN
INTERCHANGEABLE . C IS OFTEN REPLACED BY G AT THE BEGINNING OF WORDS .
B AND P CAN ALSO SWAP AND SO CAN M AND F , AND D AND T . AU , AI OR
IAU ARE USUALLY USED AT THE END OF A WORD TO MAKE IT PLURAL .

THIS LIST WILL HELP YOU UNDERSTAND SOME OF THE PLACE NAMES YOU COME
ACROSS WHILST RIDING YOUR BEIC MYNYDD IN CYMRU !

ABER – RIVER MOUTH
AFON – RIVER
ALLT – HEIGHT OR HILL

BACH – SMALL
BEDD – GRAVE
BEUDY – COW SHED
BLAEN – HEAD OF A VALLEY
BOD – DWELLING
BONT – BRIDGE
BRE – HILL
BRON OR BRYN – HILLTOP
BWLCH – MOUNTAIN PASS

CABAN – HUT
CADAIR OR CADER – SEAT
CAER – FORT
CAPEL – CHAPEL
CARN – CAIRN
CARREG – ROCK
CAS OR CASTELL – CASTLE
CEFN – RIDGE OR PATH
CLAWDD – BANK OR DYKE
COCH – RED
COED – WOOD
CRAIG – ROCK OR CRAG
CROES – CROSS

CWM – VALLEY

DDU – BLACK
DDWR , DWR OR DWFR – WATER
DEWI – (SAINT) DAVID
DIN , DINAS OR DUN – FORT
DOL – MEADOW
DRAETH – BEACH
DWY – RIVER GODDESS
DYFFRYN – VALLEY

EFAIL – SMITHY
EGLWYS – CHURCH
EPPYNT – HORSE TRACK
ESGAIR – RIDGE

FACH – SMALL
FAEN – STONE
FAWR – GREAT
FOEL – HILL OR BARREN
FFORDD – ROAD
FFRIDD OR FRIDD – MOUNTAIN PASTURE
FFYNON – SPRING OR WELL

GAER – FORT
GARN – CAIRN
GARTH – ENCLOSED HILL

54

GARW – ROUGH OR RUGGED
GLAN – RIVER BANK
GLAS – GREEN
GOED – WOOD
GROES – CROSS
GWAUN – MOOR
GWEN OR GWYN – WHITE
GWYLLT – WILD

HAFOD – SUMMER FARMHOUSE
HEN – OLD
HENDRE – WINTER FARMHOUSE
HEOL – ROAD
HIR – OLD

IS – BELOW
ISAF – LOWEST

LLAN – CHURCH
LLANFAIR – CHURCH OF SAINT MARY
LLECH – FLAT STONE
LLUEST – SHEPHERD'S HUT
LLWYBR – PATH
LLWYD – GREY
LLYN – LAKE
LLYS – COURT OR MANOR HOUSE

MA OR MAES – FIELD
MAEN – STONE
MAER – STEWARD OR LOCAL OFFICIAL
MAI – PLAIN
MARCH – HORSE
MAWR – GREAT
MELIN – MILL
MOCH – PIG
MOEL – HILL OR BARREN
MORFA – MARSH
MYNACH – MONK
MYNYDD – MOUNTAIN

NANT – STREAM OR VALLEY
NEUADD – HALL
NEWYDD – NEW

OGOF – CAVE

PANDY – FULLING MILL
PANT – HOLLOW
PEN – TOP OR HEAD
PENTRE – VILLAGE
PISTYLL – WATERFALL
PLAS – MANSION
PONT – BRIDGE
PWLL – POOL

RHAEADR – WATERFALL
RHIW – HILLSIDE
RHOS – MOOR
RHUDD – RED
RHYD – FORD

SARN – PAVED ROAD

TAL – END
TAN – BELOW
TON – MARSHY
TRAETH – BEACH
TRAWS – ACROSS
TRE OR TREF – VILLAGE OR HOME
TWMPATH – MOUND
TY – HOUSE
TYWYN – SAND DUNES

UCHAF – HIGHEST

WAEN OR WAUN – MOOR
WERN – BOG

Y – THE
YNYS – ISLAND
YSBYTY – HOSPITAL
YSTRAD – VALLEY BOTTOM

LLWYBR CEFFYL
PUBLIC BRIDLEWAY

THE VILLAGE OF CEDEWAIN CHANGED ITS NAME
TO NEWTOWN IN MEDIEVAL TIMES AS PART OF A
SCHEME TO BOOST LOCAL TRADE. IT SEEMS TO
HAVE WORKED! - NEWTOWN DEVELOPED INTO A
THRIVING MARKET TOWN AND AN IMPORTANT
CENTRE FOR THE WOOL AND FLANNEL INDUSTRIES.

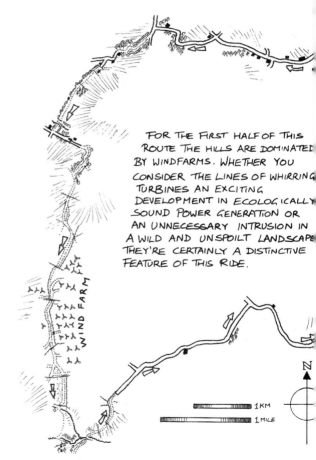

FOR THE FIRST HALF OF THIS
ROUTE THE HILLS ARE DOMINATED
BY WINDFARMS. WHETHER YOU
CONSIDER THE LINES OF WHIRRING
TURBINES AN EXCITING
DEVELOPMENT IN ECOLOGICALLY
SOUND POWER GENERATION OR
AN UNNECESSARY INTRUSION IN
A WILD AND UNSPOILT LANDSCAPE
THEY'RE CERTAINLY A DISTINCTIVE
FEATURE OF THIS RIDE.

WIND FARM

N

1 KM

1 MILE

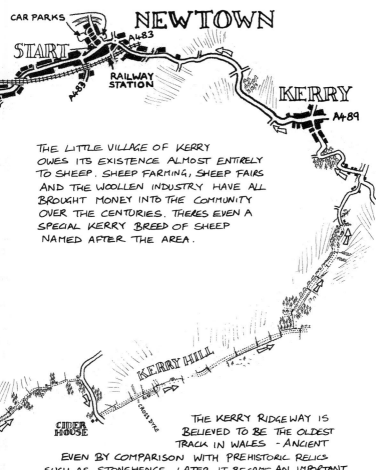

CAR PARKS

NEWTOWN

START

A483

RAILWAY STATION

A483

KERRY

A489

THE LITTLE VILLAGE OF KERRY OWES ITS EXISTENCE ALMOST ENTIRELY TO SHEEP. SHEEP FARMING, SHEEP FAIRS AND THE WOOLLEN INDUSTRY HAVE ALL BROUGHT MONEY INTO THE COMMUNITY OVER THE CENTURIES. THERES EVEN A SPECIAL KERRY BREED OF SHEEP NAMED AFTER THE AREA.

KERRY HILL

CROSS DYKE

CIDER HOUSE

THE KERRY RIDGEWAY IS BELIEVED TO BE THE OLDEST TRACK IN WALES - ANCIENT EVEN BY COMPARISON WITH PREHISTORIC RELICS SUCH AS STONEHENGE. LATER IT BECAME AN IMPORTANT ROUTE FOR DROVERS, BRINGING CATTLE AND SHEEP FROM FARMS WEST OF LLANIDLOES OVER KERRY HILL TO BISHOPS CASTLE AND ACROSS SHROPSHIRE TO THE MARKETS OF THE MIDLANDS.

KERRY HILL

ROUTE 8

MAP: LANDRANGER 136 MOST OF THE ROUTE IS ALSO ON PATHFINDER 929
DISTANCE: 26½ MILES / 43 KM   OFFROAD: 12 MILES / 19 KM
TIME: 3½ – 5 HOURS
HIGHEST POINT: 1745 FT / 532 M
TOTAL CLIMBING: 3000 FT / 900 M
START: NEWTOWN   109 914

FROM THE CENTRE OF NEWTOWN MAKE YOUR WAY TO THE A483/A489 AND
TURN WEST. ROLL OUT OF TOWN HEADING STRAIGHT ALONG THE ROAD UNTIL SHORTLY
AFTER PASSING UNDER A BRIDGE YOU REACH A ROUNDABOUT. TURN LEFT AND THEN
RIGHT AT THE NEXT ROUNDABOUT. AFTER ¾ MILE (1KM) YOU COME TO THE LITTLE VILLAGE
OF STEPASIDE WHERE YOU SHOULD TURN RIGHT UP A SMALL ROAD SIGNED TO
CAERSWS. CLIMB GENTLY FOR 2½ MILES (4KM) UNTIL AT THE TOP OF THE HILL
YOU REACH A SORT OF T-JUNCTION – THE ROAD ACTUALLY CONTINUES ROUND TO THE
RIGHT BUT YOU NEED TO TURN OFF LEFT.

AFTER 200 YARDS SWING RIGHT OFF THE ROAD ONTO A GOOD TRACK. THIS BECOMES
A STEEP, FAST DESCENT WITH SHARP BENDS AND BIG RAMPS. KEEP GOING AT
THE BOTTOM WHERE THE TRACK BECOMES TARMAC THEN TURN LEFT WHEN YOU
REACH A RED TELEPHONE BOX. AT THE TOP OF A SHORT CLIMB GO THROUGH A
GATE AND STRAIGHT ON PAST CROSS KEYS COTTAGE (MIND THE DUCKS!).
ANOTHER GATE, BEYOND THE COTTAGE, TAKES YOU ONTO A GRASSY PATH ALONG
THE BOTTOM OF A STEEP HILLSIDE. FOLLOW THE PATH BESIDE THE FENCE FOR
1 MILE (1.5 KM), THROUGH A COUPLE OF GATES AND EVENTUALLY TO A DARK, MUDDY
LANE. CROSS THE ROCKY FORD (OR WIMP OUT AND USE THE LITTLE BRIDGE)
THEN SLITHER YOUR WAY UP THE MUDDY SLOPE BEYOND.

TURN LEFT WHEN YOU REACH THE ROAD AND FOLLOW THE TARMAC UP THE VALLEY.
AT THE END OF THE ROAD CONTINUE UP A GOOD STONY TRACK. KEEP CLIMBING
UNTIL YOU EVENTUALLY REACH A T-JUNCTION. TURN LEFT, THROUGH THE GATE
AND CONTINUE UP WHAT IS BY NOW BECOMING A REAL LUNG BURSTER OF A
CLIMB. AFTER ANOTHER GATE FORK LEFT AND THEN, FURTHER ON, RIGHT.
STICK TO THE BIGGEST OF THE TRACKS AND KEEP BATTLING YOUR WAY UPWARDS
UNTIL THE TRACK EVENTUALLY SWINGS LEFT TO MEET A FENCE. EVEN IF THE
MONSTER CLIMB HASN'T COMPLETELY EXHAUSTED YOU IT'S WORTH STOPPING HERE
FOR A FEW MINUTES REST JUST SO YOU CAN GAWP AT THE BRILLIANT VIEWS.

AFTER YOU'VE RESTED CONTINUE ALONG THE TRACK, WITH THE FENCE ON YOUR LEFT,
HEADING TOWARDS THE WIND FARM. WHEN YOU REACH A GATE GO THROUGH AND
CONTINUE, WITH THE FENCE ON YOUR RIGHT, PAST WHIRLING WIND TURBINES TO
MEET A WELL SURFACED TRACK. GO THROUGH A GATE AND HEAD STRAIGHT

ON, IGNORING SERVICE TRACKS OFF TO THE WINDMILLS ON EITHER SIDE, THEN FORKING LEFT WHERE A BRANCH OF THE TRACK SWINGS RIGHT, DOWN TOWARDS THE VALLEY. GO THROUGH A GATE, FORK LEFT AGAIN AND THEN FURTHER ON WHERE THE TRACK BENDS TO THE LEFT SWING OFF ONTO THE GRASS, GOING STRAIGHT ON, ACROSS ANOTHER TRACK TO A FENCE. (THIS SECTION IS A BIT TRICKY AS THERE IS NO OBVIOUS TRACK. HOPEFULLY THINGS SHOULD SOON BE IMPROVED THOUGH- SO LOOK OUT FOR NEW SIGN POSTS ETC.) CLIMB OVER THE FENCE AND GO STRAIGHT ON ACROSS THE ROUGH GROUND KEEPING PARALLEL TO A FENCE (AND A SMOOTH CLEAR TRACK!) ABOUT 50 YARDS TO YOUR LEFT. EVENTUALLY YOU MEET THE TRACK BY A GATE. GO THROUGH AND FOLLOW A FAINT TRACK FOR 1/3 MILE (0.5 KM) LEADING TO AN EMBANKMENT ACROSS A ROCKY RAVINE. GO UP THE SLOPE BEYOND AND THROUGH A SMALL GATE BY SOME RUINED BARNS SURROUNDED BY TREES. TURN LEFT BY THE BARNS AND ROLL DOWN THE FIELD TO A TRACK.

TURN LEFT AND FOLLOW THE TRACK. IT PASSES THROUGH VARIOUS GATES, GRADUALLY GETTING BETTER DEFINED UNTIL AFTER ABOUT A MILE (1.5 KM) IT BECOMES TARMAC. CRUISE ON STRAIGHT DOWN THE ROAD UNTIL YOU EVENTUALLY REACH A T-JUNCTION. TURN RIGHT AND CONTINUE UNTIL YOU COME TO ANOTHER T-JUNCTION. TURN RIGHT, AND THEN AFTER 200 YARDS TURN LEFT ONTO AN OBVIOUS TRACK, THROUGH A GATE.

FOLLOW THIS TRACK FOR 2 MILES (3 KM) GOING THROUGH VARIOUS GATES AND PASSING A FEW OLD BARNS. WHEN YOU EVENTUALLY REACH TARMAC AGAIN TURN RIGHT. AFTER 1/2 MILE (0.75 KM) TURN LEFT ONTO A TRACK OPPOSITE CIDER HOUSE. THIS FARM WAS ONCE A DROVERS' INN, BUT IS NOW DERELICT. (PITY - YOU'LL PROBABLY QUITE FANCY A PINT OR TWO OF CIDER BY THE TIME YOU GET HERE!)

THE ROUTE NOW IS PART OF THE ANCIENT KERRY RIDGEWAY. THE TRACK HEADS OVER THE HILLTOP IN A STRAIGHT LINE, CLIMBING GENTLY THROUGH VARIOUS GATES AND GRADUALLY BECOMING LESS WELL DEFINED - ALTHOUGH THERE ARE BRIDLEWAY BADGES ON ALL THE GATES TO KEEP YOU HEADING THE RIGHT WAY. (AFTER A COUPLE OF GATES LOOK OUT FOR A CROSS DYKE - THIS WAS ONCE A DEFENSIVE BOUNDARY, PROBABLY MARKING THE EDGE OF A PREHISTORIC RANCH. JUST BEYOND, LOOK FOR A COUPLE OF GRASSY MOUNDS - KNOWN AS THE TWO TUMPS. PREHISTORIC IN ORIGIN, THESE WERE LATER USED AS A MEETING POINT FOR DROVERS - GATHERING TOGETHER HUGE FLOCKS AND HERDS BEFORE MARCHING EAST ALONG THE RIDGEWAY.) WHERE THE TRACK FADES OUT KEEP GOING STRAIGHT ON UNTIL YOU PICK UP A GRASSY TRACK. THIS BECOMES GRAVELLY AND FAST PAST SOME FELLED FOREST ON YOUR RIGHT AND THROUGH SOME GATES. PASS SOME FOREST ON YOUR LEFT AND AT THE END OF IT TURN LEFT OFF THE KERRY RIDGEWAY, THROUGH A SMALL GATE INTO A FIELD. FOLLOW THE EDGE OF THE FIELD DOWN TO A TRACK BEARING SLIGHTLY RIGHT THROUGH A GAP IN THE FOREST. FROM HERE THE TRACK IS OBVIOUS ALL THE WAY DOWN THE HILL, THROUGH A FEW GATES AND EVENTUALLY OUT ONTO TARMAC BY A FARMHOUSE. (THE FINAL SECTION OF SUNKEN LANE IS OVERGROWN - SO USE THE FIELD EDGE TO THE RIGHT OF IT.)

CONTINUE DOWN THE ROAD UNTIL YOU REACH A T-JUNCTION. TURN LEFT AND THEN, AFTER 150 YARDS, LEFT AGAIN. THIS ROAD TWISTS AROUND THE HILL AND THEN DROPS DOWN INTO KERRY. TURN LEFT ONTO THE MAIN ROAD BACK TO NEWTOWN.

THINGS TO SEE ~ Historic Tracks

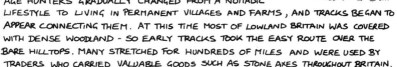

Scooting across the hills on your state of the art bike you may be surprised to find you could be following a route that's so old it makes Stonehenge look new-fangled and modern! The first tracks probably appeared in Wales about 8000 years ago. Stone Age hunters gradually changed from a nomadic lifestyle to living in permanent villages and farms, and tracks began to appear connecting them. At this time most of lowland Britain was covered with dense woodland - so early tracks took the easy route over the bare hilltops. Many stretched for hundreds of miles and were used by traders who carried valuable goods such as stone axes throughout Britain.

As the population increased, the trees were cleared to make way for fields, and tracks spread down into the sheltered valleys. By the Iron Age - 2000 years ago - the country would have been covered with an extensive network of twisting muddy roads. Then the Romans arrived, bringing armies of organised road builders and new ideas such as paving stones and straight lines. (Although the Welsh hills played hell with their straight roads!) Soldiers and merchants were able to move swiftly throughout Wales and the Marches. When the Romans finally left, the roads rapidly fell into disrepair and for over 1000 years few people in mid-Wales would have travelled far beyond their nearest village. But this isolation helped to preserve the Celtic culture from many of the changes happening elsewhere in Britain.

As well as monks and merchants (carrying their goods by packhorse) one of the few groups of travellers in medieval Wales were drovers. They collected livestock from farms and marched them hundreds of miles to markets in London and the Midlands. (Devices for protecting animals' feet included metal shoes for cattle, leather socks for pigs and geeses' feet were dipped in tar.) The drovers used special tracks across the bare hilltops - to avoid causing chaos in the valleys. But the wild hills were also the lair of outlaws who would attack the drovers when they returned with their profits from the markets.

Today many roads have been covered with tarmac for use by cars. But thousands of miles of ancient routes - originally used by travellers on foot or horse back - still survive as bridleways and other rights of way.

STAYLITTLE'S ORIGINAL WELSH NAME WAS PENFFORDDLAS – MEANING THE END OF THE GREEN LANE – WHICH MAKES IT SOUND IDEAL AS THE STARTING PLACE FOR A MOUNTAIN BIKE RIDE! (IT WAS ACTUALLY NAMED AFTER THE END OF A DROVERS' ROAD.)

STAYLITTLE

PARKING SPACE

START

B4518

AFON TWYMYN

PENYCROCBREN

DYLIFE

MINE RUINS

LLYN GLASLYN

FOEL FADIAN

ABERHOSAN

NEWTOWN

A470

LLANIDLOES

STAYLITTLE

DYLIFE

LLYN CLYWEDOG

LLANIDLOES

MACHYNLLETH

N

1 KM
1 MILE

BEYOND FOEL FADIAN THE TYPICAL BLEAK MOORLAND THROWS IN A SURPRISE – BY STOPPING. THE DESCENT FROM THE HILL INTO THE VALLEYS BEYOND IS SERIOUSLY GNARLY – AND SERIOUSLY BRILLIANT. (DEFINITELY THE HIGHLIGHT OF THIS RIDE – IF NOT YOUR WHOLE YEAR!)

FOEL FADIAN

MAP: LANDRANGERS 135 OR 136   PATHFINDER 907
DISTANCE: 15½ MILES /24.5 KM   OFFROAD: 9½ MILES /15.5 KM
TIME: 2 – 4 HOURS
HIGHEST POINT: 1675 FT /510 M
TOTAL CLIMBING: 2800 FT /850 M
START: STAYLITTLE   884 924

THE BEST STARTING POINT IS AT THE BOTTOM OF THE LANE IN
STAYLITTLE. THERE IS ENOUGH SPACE FOR 2 OR 3 CARS TO PARK
WHERE THE LANE MEETS THE B4518. ALTERNATIVELY TRY PARKING
AT DYLIFE AND FOLLOW THE ROAD ROUND TO THE START.

FROM THE START FOLLOW THE LITTLE ROAD NORTH-WEST FOR ¾ MILE
(1KM). WHERE THE TARMAC SWINGS LEFT TO A FARMHOUSE CARRY ON
STRAIGHT AHEAD ON THE OBVIOUS TRACK. THIS TRACK IS PART OF
GLYNDWR'S WAY AND IS WELL WAYMARKED. FOLLOW THE GATED TRACK
ACROSS BLEAK MOORLAND FIELDS. IGNORE THE BRIDLEWAY SIGNPOSTED TO THE
RIGHT AFTER 1 MILE (1.5KM) AND CONTINUE OVER PENYCROCBREN. THE TOP OF
THIS HILL WAS CROWNED BY A SMALL FORT IN ROMAN TIMES – AND IN THE
18TH CENTURY WAS THE SITE OF A GALLOWS. (AN EERIE SPOT ON A
MISTY DAY!)

WHEN YOU REACH ANOTHER TRACK TURN LEFT. TAKE THE RIGHT FORK
AFTER ABOUT 100 YARDS AND CONTINUE TO A GATE. DON'T GO THROUGH
THE GATE ON THE TRACK – BUT TURN RIGHT THROUGH A GATE INTO A FIELD
AND RIDE UP THE HILLSIDE. THERE IS NO TRACK VISIBLE – SO KEEP THE
FENCE ON YOUR RIGHT AND FOLLOW IT TO THE TOP. WHEN YOU COME TO
ANOTHER FENCE GO THROUGH THE GATE AND BEAR LEFT. LOOK FOR A LOW
EARTH BANK WHICH YOU SHOULD THEN FOLLOW. A TINY PATH GRADUALLY
APPEARS BY THE BANK. CONTINUE ALONG THE TRACK A LITTLE FURTHER ON,
WHERE IT SWINGS ACROSS THE HILLSIDE AWAY FROM THE EARTH BANK. CROSS
A STILE AND FOLLOW THE PATH TO A STEEP LITTLE VALLEY AT THE
JUNCTION OF TWO STREAMS. THE SHORT DESCENT TO THE STREAM IS
TRICKY – WITH A STEEP DROP ON ONE SIDE (IF IN DOUBT – WALK IT).

CROSS THE FOOTBRIDGE AND CARRY YOUR BIKE UP THE OPPOSITE SLOPE
(UNLESS YOU HAVE SUPER HUMAN BIKE SKILLS!) PASS TO THE RIGHT
OF THE BARN AND SHEEP PENS AND JOIN THE GOOD STONY TRACK.
RIDE UP THE BRIDLEWAY FOR ¾ MILE (1KM), TURN RIGHT AT A T-JUNCTION
AND CONTINUE PAST A LAKE. ABOUT ⅓ MILE (0.5KM) PAST THE
LAKE YOU'LL SEE A TRACK LEADING OFF UP THE HILL AHEAD OF

63

YOU. TURN LEFT ONTO IT - HEADING TOWARDS FOEL FADIAN.

AFTER A BIT OF GENTLE CLIMBING THIS TRACK SWINGS LEFT AND
TURNS INTO A TRULY AWESOME DESCENT. HEWN ROUGHLY FROM THE
BEDROCK, IT IS 100% RIDEABLE - BUT NEEDS 100% CONCENTRATION.
(IT'S WORTH STOPPING A FEW TIMES FOR THE VIEWS - THE BARE SCREE
SLOPES OF THE VALLEY ON YOUR LEFT ARE PRETTY AMAZING.) TURN
LEFT PART OF THE WAY DOWN AND HOLD ON TIGHT AS YOU PLUMMET
DOWN A SERIES OF STEEP ZIGZAGS. FURTHER DOWN THE TRACK
GETS SMOOTHER AND FASTER (WATCH OUT FOR WALKERS, SHEEP
AND GATES) EVENTUALLY BRINGING YOU TO A FARM 1½ MILES (2.5 KM)
HORIZONTALLY AND 1150 FT (350 M) VERTICALLY FROM THE TOP.
DROP DOWN THROUGH A SECOND FARM AND ONTO TARMAC. TURN RIGHT UP
A SLOPE AND FOLLOW THE ROAD FOR 1 MILE (1.5 KM) DOWN TO ABERHOSAN.

TURN RIGHT JUST BEFORE THE CHAPEL. THIS IS WHERE YOU
START PAYING FOR THAT MAGIC DESCENT. THE ROAD CLIMBS
STEADILY PAST SOME HOUSES (IGNORE TURNINGS TO THE LEFT OR
RIGHT) FOR ABOUT ⅓ MILE (0.5 KM) UNTIL THE TARMAC FADES OUT.
CONTINUE UP THE CLEAR TRACK, WHICH AFTER A MILE (1.5 KM) REACHES
A FOREST. CONTINUE CLIMBING BESIDE THE TREES (THIS BIT IS
STEEP) UNTIL YOU FINALLY REACH THE ROAD. THE VIEWPOINT AT
THE TOP OF THE TRACK (A MEMORIAL TO THE WRITER AND BROADCASTER
WYNFORD VAUGHAN-THOMAS) IS AN IDEAL PLACE TO COLLAPSE AND
GET YOUR BREATH BACK.

TURN RIGHT ONTO THE TARMAC AND FOLLOW IT FOR 2½ MILES (4KM),
ACROSS THE HILLTOP AND DOWN TO DYLIFE. DYLIFE WAS ONCE A
PROSPEROUS MINING VILLAGE. A FEW REMAINS OF THE OLD MINES CAN
STILL BE SEEN ON THE SURROUNDING HILLS, BUT THE VILLAGE IS NOW
NO MORE THAN A HANDFUL OF HOUSES AND A PUB.

HERE YOU HAVE A CHOICE. TO FOLLOW THE MAIN ROUTE, TURN RIGHT
ONTO A TRACK - JUST PAST THE JUNCTION FOR THE ROAD TO THE PUB. A
SHORT CLIMB TAKES YOU BACK UP TO THE GLYNDŴR'S WAY TRACK
FROM STAYLITTLE. TURN LEFT AND FOLLOW THE TRACK AND THEN ROAD
BACK DOWN TO THE START.

ALTERNATIVELY YOU COULD CONTINUE ALONG THE ROAD FOR 1½ MILES
(2.5 KM) AND THEN TURN RIGHT AT THE T-JUNCTION AND FOLLOW THE
B4518 FOR 1 MILE (1.5 KM) BACK TO THE START. THIS WAY YOU CAN
HAVE A GAWP AT THE VIEW DOWN THE TWYMYN VALLEY WITH ITS
DRAMATIC WATERFALL AND CLIFFS.

THE GREAT MASS OF THE LONGMYND DOMINATES
CHURCH STRETTON. REACHING THE WILD MOORLAND
OF THE SUMMIT PLATEAU INVOLVES SOME
STEEP CLIMBING. SUPERB VIEWS AND
BRILLIANT DESCENTS ARE THE REWARD
FOR YOUR HARD WORK.

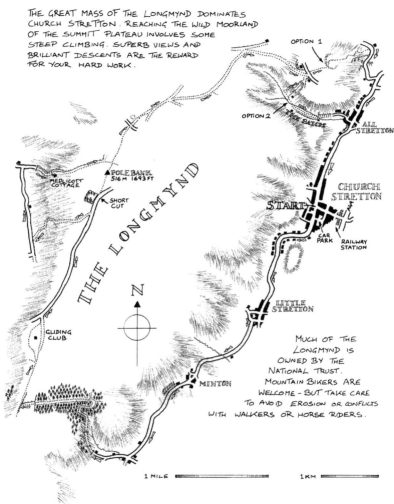

OPTION 1

OPTION 2

THE BATCH

ALL
STRETTON

POLE BANK
516 M 1693 FT

MEDLICOTT
COTTAGE

SHORT
CUT

CHURCH
STRETTON

START

CAR
PARK

RAILWAY
STATION

THE LONGMYND

N

LITTLE
STRETTON

GLIDING
CLUB

MINTON

MUCH OF THE
LONGMYND IS
OWNED BY THE
NATIONAL TRUST.
MOUNTAIN BIKERS ARE
WELCOME - BUT TAKE CARE
TO AVOID EROSION OR CONFLICTS
WITH WALKERS OR HORSE RIDERS.

1 MILE

1 KM

THE LONGMYND

MAP: LANDRANGER 137. MOST OF THE ROUTE IS ALSO SHOWN ON PATHFINDER 910
DISTANCE: 20 MILES / 32 KM   OFFROAD: 9 MILES / 15 KM
TIME: 2½ - 3½ HOURS
HIGHEST POINT: 1695 FT / 516 M
TOTAL CLIMBING: 2000 FT / 600 M - OR 1350 FT / 400 M VIA SHORT CUT
START: CHURCH STRETTON   454 936

FROM THE CENTRE OF CHURCH STRETTON TAKE THE ROAD TO LITTLE
STRETTON. IN THE VILLAGE TURN RIGHT OPPOSITE THE THATCHED HALF-
TIMBERED CHURCH (SUPPLIED IN KIT FORM BY A BIRMINGHAM COMPANY
IN 1903!). BEAR LEFT, THEN RIGHT UP A NARROW ROAD FOR A MILE
(1.5 KM), THROUGH A FORD AND UP THE STEEP CLIMB TO MINTON.

AFTER MINTON CONTINUE FOR ANOTHER MILE AND A HALF (2.5 KM) TO A CROSSROADS
AND TURN RIGHT. THIS ROAD LEADS TO A WIDE TRACK CLIMBING UP THROUGH A FOREST.
1½ MILES (3 KM) OF SLOG TAKE YOU UP ONTO THE LONGMYND'S MOORLAND
PLATEAU. PASS THROUGH A GATE AT THE TOP OF THE FOREST AND CONTINUE TO
ANOTHER GATE.

TURN RIGHT TOWARDS THE GLIDING CLUB. THE BRIDLEWAY ACTUALLY CROSSES THE
AIRFIELD BUT THE DIVERSION - MARKED BY SMALL WHITE POSTS - KEEPS OUT OF
THE WAY OF GLIDERS AND HAS BETTER VIEWS. OUT OF THE GLIDING CLUB GATES
TURN RIGHT ON THE ROAD. AFTER 1½ MILES (2 KM) TURN LEFT ONTO A TRACK
JUST BEFORE A SMALL WOODED ENCLOSURE. (FOR A SHORT CUT - MISSING
OUT THE 600 FT (200 M) DESCENT AND CLIMB, CONTINUE ALONG THE ROAD
AND BEAR LEFT SHORTLY AFTER THE ENCLOSURE, UP THE LITTLE TRACK TO
POLE BANK - THE SUMMIT OF THE LONGMYND).

THE TRACK DOWN THE WEST SIDE OF THE LONGMYND HAS JUST THE
RIGHT AMOUNT OF STEEPNESS, ROUGHNESS AND TWISTYNESS FOR A
BRILLIANT BULGING EYEBALLS AND MANIC GRIN DESCENT. TURN RIGHT ALONG
THE LITTLE ROAD AT THE BOTTOM. AFTER A MILE (1.5 KM) TURN RIGHT UP A
STEEP ROAD WITH A DEAD END SIGN AT THE BOTTOM. THE TARMAC
GRADUALLY FADES TO BECOME A MOORLAND TRACK AT MEDLICOTT
COTTAGE. CONTINUE UNTIL YOU MEET ANOTHER TRACK CROSSING THE ONE
YOU'RE ON. TURN RIGHT UP TO THE SUMMIT TRIG POINT. ON A CLEAR
DAY THE VIEWS ARE FANTASTIC - FROM THE TOWER BLOCKS OF WOLVERHAMPTON
TO THE BRECON BEACONS AND THE PEAKS OF SNOWDONIA.

FROM THE SUMMIT, RIDE BACK DOWN THE TRACK YOU JUST CAME UP (OR
CONTINUE STRAIGHT AHEAD IF YOU TOOK THE SHORT CUT.) CROSS STRAIGHT
OVER THE TRACK FROM MEDLICOTT COTTAGE AND CONTINUE NORTH-EAST
ALONG THE HILLTOP. AFTER CROSSING A ROAD THE TRACK SPLITS

INTO 2 OR 3 PARALLEL PATHS – DON'T WORRY THEY ALL CONVERGE AGAIN FURTHER ON. THIS ROUTE ALONG THE TOP OF THE LONGMYND, CALLED THE PORTWAY, IS A PREHISTORIC TRACKWAY WHICH HAS PROBABLY BEEN IN USE FOR OVER 3000 YEARS.

ABOUT ½ MILE (0·8KM) AFTER CROSSING THE ROAD YOU PASS A SMALL SIGN POST MARKING THE ROUTE DOWN TO CARDINGMILL VALLEY. IGNORE THIS TRACK – BUT BEAR RIGHT BETWEEN THE CARDINGMILL TRACK AND THE ROUTE YOU'RE ON. AFTER A FEW MINUTES THIS TRACK BEGINS TO GENTLY DESCEND. JUST BEFORE REACHING A FENCE AT THE EDGE OF THE MOORLAND TURN RIGHT DOWN A SMOOTH GRASSY SLOPE ON A VAGUE TRACK. HALFWAY DOWN YOU PASS THROUGH A CROSS DIKE – ANOTHER PREHISTORIC RELIC, PROBABLY BUILT AS A CATTLE RANCH BOUNDARY BY BRONZE AGE FARMERS. AT THE BOTTOM THE TRACK GETS ROUGH, PASSING TO THE RIGHT OF A HOUSE JUST BEFORE MEETING THE ROAD. YOU NOW HAVE A CHOICE OF TWO EXCELLENT DESCENTS.

OPTION 1. TURN LEFT UP THE ROAD FOR 100 YARDS THEN TURN RIGHT ONTO A FAINT TRACK. THIS IS ONLY A PERMISSIVE BRIDLEWAY AND IS POPULAR WITH HORSE RIDERS – SO PLEASE RIDE WITH CARE. AFTER A GENTLE START THIS BECOMES A BRILLIANT ROLLER COASTER RIDE – FAST AND TWISTY. A REAL ADRENALIN RUSH. TURN RIGHT ON THE ROAD AT THE BOTTOM AND FOLLOW IT TO A T-JUNCTION. TURN RIGHT AGAIN FOR THE 2 MILE (3KM) CRUISE BACK THROUGH ALL STRETTON TO CHURCH STRETTON.

OPTION 2. THIS ROUTE TAKES YOU DOWN INTO THE PICTURESQUE BATCH VALLEY VIA A STEEP AND VERY NARROW TRACK. JUST BEFORE THE ROAD, TURN RIGHT AND SKIRT ROUND TO THE RIGHT OF A BOGGY PATCH TO WHERE A LITTLE STREAM DROPS DOWN INTO A MINIATURE VALLEY. THE PATH DROPS DOWN FOLLOWING THE STREAM, VIA A STEEP, NARROW LEDGE ACROSS THE FACE OF A ROCK OUTCROP, WITH A NASTY DROP BENEATH YOUR LEFT PEDAL. IF YOU KEEP A COOL HEAD IT'S FAIRLY EASY – BUT TAKE A LOOK ON FOOT FIRST IF YOU'RE NOT TOO SURE. THE LITTLE VALLEY SUDDENLY ENDS HIGH UP THE SIDE OF THE MAIN BATCH VALLEY. WHILE THE STREAM PLUNGES STRAIGHT DOWN, THE PATH SWINGS RIGHT AND TAKES A (SLIGHTLY) MORE GENTLE ROUTE DOWN. AT THE BOTTOM TURN LEFT AND CRUISE DOWN THE VALLEY. THE TRACK GRADUALLY BECOMES BETTER DEFINED, PASSES THROUGH A COUPLE OF FORDS AND EVENTUALLY BECOMES TARMAC ON THE EDGE OF ALL STRETTON. ROLL DOWN TO A T-JUNCTION AND TURN RIGHT BACK TO CHURCH STRETTON.

FOR A WELL EARNED DRINK OF FRESH SPRING WATER STOP AT THE CWM DALE BOTTLING FACTORY ON THE ROAD BACK TO CHURCH STRETTON AND REFILL YOUR BOTTLES FROM THE TAP IN THE WALL.

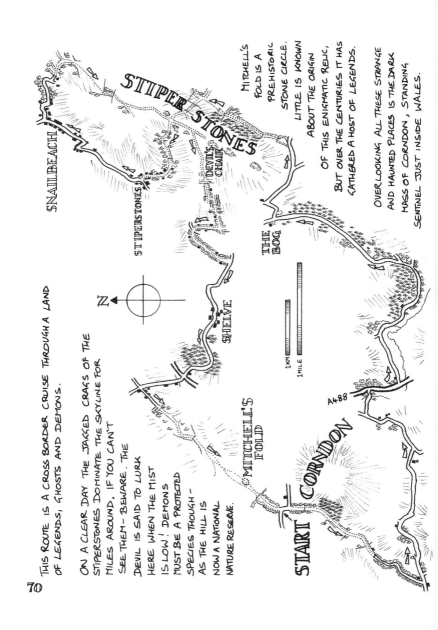

THIS ROUTE IS A CROSS BORDER CRUISE THROUGH A LAND OF LEGENDS, GHOSTS AND DEMONS.

ON A CLEAR DAY THE JAGGED CRAGS OF THE STIPERSTONES DOMINATE THE SKYLINE FOR MILES AROUND. IF YOU CAN'T SEE THEM – BEWARE. THE DEVIL IS SAID TO LURK HERE WHEN THE MIST IS LOW! DEMONS MUST BE A PROTECTED SPECIES THOUGH – AS THE HILL IS NOW A NATIONAL NATURE RESERVE.

MITCHELL'S FOLD IS A PREHISTORIC STONE CIRCLE. LITTLE IS KNOWN ABOUT THE ORIGIN OF THIS ENIGMATIC RELIC, BUT OVER THE CENTURIES IT HAS GATHERED A HOST OF LEGENDS.

OVERLOOKING ALL THESE STRANGE AND HAUNTED PLACES IS THE DARK MASS OF CORNDON, STANDING SENTINEL JUST INSIDE WALES.

SNAILBEACH

STIPER STONES

DEVIL'S CHAIR

STIPERSTONES

N

THE BOG

SHELVE

1 KM

1 MILE

A488

MITCHELL'S FOLD

START CORNDON

THE STIPERSTONES

MAP: LANDRANGERS 126 + 137   OR PATHFINDERS 888 + 909
DISTANCE: 25 MILES / 40 KM   OFFROAD: 10½ MILES / 17 KM
TIME: 2½ – 4½ HOURS
HIGHEST POINT: 1600 FT / 490 M
TOTAL CLIMBING: 3300 FT / 1000 M
START: END OF TRACK TO MITCHELL'S FOLD 302977

HEAD SOUTH DOWN THE ROAD FOR 100 YARDS AND STRAIGHT UP A WELL
MADE TRACK. GENTLE CLIMBING TAKES YOU PAST CORNDON BEFORE DROPPING
DOWN THE FAR SIDE – WITH SUPERB VIEWS OUT TO THE WEST. BEYOND A COTTAGE THE
TRACK BECOMES TARMAC AND YOU ZIP DOWN TO A T-JUNCTION. TURN LEFT ALONG THE
ROAD, DOWN INTO A VALLEY AND UP THE STEEP CLIMB BEYOND. THE NEXT FEW MILES
ARE ALL ON TARMAC (MOSTLY SMALL COUNTRY LANES). AFTER THE CLIMB KEEP
GOING UNTIL YOU EVENTUALLY REACH A T-JUNCTION. TURN LEFT, AND THEN RIGHT
AFTER 1 MILE (1·5 KM). DROP DOWN TO THE A488, TURN RIGHT AND THEN LEFT
AFTER ⅓ MILE (0·5 KM) - SIGNED TO NIND. CRUISE ALONG THE VALLEY (THERE ARE
SOME ACE CLIMBING TREES ALONG THE ROADSIDE!), EVENTUALLY BEARING LEFT-
SIGNED TO THE BOG AND STIPERSTONES. CLIMB UP THROUGH THE FOREST AND
ALONG THE TOP TO THE OLD MINING RUINS AT THE BOG. TURN RIGHT AND HEAD UP THE
HILL. TURN LEFT AFTER ¾ MILE (1 KM) AND LEFT AGAIN ½ MILE (0·7 KM) FURTHER ON
INTO THE STIPERSTONES NATURE RESERVE CAR PARK.

AT THE FAR END OF THE CAR PARK GO THROUGH A GATE AND CONTINUE ALONG A TRACK
TO, AND THEN ALONGSIDE A FOREST. AT THE FAR END OF THE TREES KEEP GOING UNTIL
YOU REACH A JUNCTION AND SWING LEFT UP THE HILL TO A GATE. GO THROUGH AND
CLIMB TO ANOTHER GATE, INTO THE NATURE RESERVE. GO THROUGH AND BEAR
RIGHT, CLIMBING UP THE TRACK ACROSS RUGGED MOORLAND. TO YOUR LEFT YOU CAN
(HOPEFULLY!) SEE THE SUMMIT CRAGS - INCLUDING THE DEVIL'S CHAIR. AS WELL
AS FOR THE DEVIL, THE STIPERSTONES ARE SAID TO BE A RESTING PLACE FOR WILD EDRIC
AND HIS ARMY OF SAXON WARRIORS, WHO WILL AWAKE FROM THEIR SLUMBERS AND
RIDE TO THE RESCUE IN TIMES OF NATIONAL PERIL!

GO STRAIGHT ON AT THE JUNCTION ON THE HILLTOP (OR LEFT IF YOU WANT
TO CUT OUT THE LOOP TO SNAILBEACH). THIS TRACK BECOMES AN EXCELLENT
STEEP, TECHNICAL DESCENT INTO PERKINS BEACH. (NO ITS NOT BY THE
SEASIDE - 'BEACH' OR 'BATCH' ARE LOCAL NAMES FOR A STEEP, NARROW VALLEY.)
FOLLOW THE OBVIOUS TRACK, SWINGING RIGHT AND THEN LEFT HALFWAY DOWN. EVENTUALLY
YOU GO THROUGH A GATE AND CONTINUE STRAIGHT DOWN A LANE (NOTE THE SIGN
WARNING CYCLISTS TO GO SLOW), PAST SOME HOUSES AND DOWN TO THE ROAD IN
STIPERSTONES VILLAGE.

TURN RIGHT (OR LEFT TO THE PUB!) AND RIDE THE 1½ MILES (2.5KM) TO SNAILBEACH (SURELY THE SILLIEST VILLAGE NAME IN SHROPSHIRE!) JUST AFTER THE VILLAGE HALL TURN RIGHT UP THE ROAD SIGNED TO LORDSHILL. CLIMB PAST MINE RUINS AND THE ENGINE SHED OF THE OLD SNAILBEACH RAILWAY. (SCENE OF THE MYSTERIOUS DISAPPEARANCE OF A STEAM LOCOMOTIVE. PROBABLY NOT THE WORK OF DEMONS SPIRITING IT AWAY TO THE UNDERWORLD - MORE LIKELY IT WAS DISMANTLED AND THE PIECES DROPPED DOWN AN OLD MINE SHAFT BY ITS ECCENTRIC DRIVER AFTER HE GOT ANNOYED WITH IT!)

AT THE TOP OF THE HILL THE ROAD SWINGS SHARPLY ROUND TO THE RIGHT. AT A JUNCTION TURN LEFT DOWN TO A GATE. GO THROUGH AND CONTINUE ON A TRACK, BEARING RIGHT AT A FORK, AND CLIMB UP TO A JUNCTION. TURN RIGHT AND FOLLOW THE TRACK UP THE HILL BETWEEN FIELDS, THEN UP THE FIELD BEYOND - AIMING FOR A GAP IN THE STRIP OF FOREST AHEAD. GO THROUGH THE GAP AND CROSS THE NEXT FIELD TO A GATE IN THE CORNER LEADING TO A WALLED LANE. AT THE TOP OF THE LANE YOU EMERGE ONTO OPEN MOORLAND AND FOLLOW THE CLEAR TRACK ALONG THE HILLTOP FOR ¾ MILE (1KM) TO THE JUNCTION WHERE YOU EARLIER WENT DOWN INTO PERKINS BEACH.

CONTINUE ALONG THE TOP OF THE HILL, PAST SOME SMALL CRAGS, ON A DEVILISHLY ROCKY TRACK. TURN RIGHT AT THE NEXT JUNCTION AND RATTLE DOWNHILL FOR ¾ MILE (1KM) TO A GATE AND A LANE BEYOND. DOWN THE LANE TURN LEFT PAST A HOUSE, THEN RIGHT. DROP DOWN THE TRACK, IGNORING ANY TURNS UNTIL, AFTER A BUNGALOW ON THE RIGHT YOU TURN RIGHT AT THE NEXT JUNCTION. FOLLOW THIS TRACK TO A T-JUNCTION.

TURN LEFT ONTO THE ROAD AND THEN GO STRAIGHT ACROSS TO A TRACK WHERE THE ROAD BENDS TO THE LEFT. FOLLOW THIS TRACK UNTIL YOU REACH TARMAC AGAIN AND THEN TURN RIGHT. CRUISE ALONG THE TARMAC FOR 2 MILES (3KM), THROUGH SHELVE AND ALONG TO A CROSSROADS. GO STRAIGHT ACROSS, THEN AFTER A LONG STRETCH OF STRAIGHT ROAD TURN LEFT. AT THE END OF THIS ROAD CONTINUE PAST A BARRIER AND ALONG A GRAVEL TRACK THROUGH CLEAR FELLED FORESTRY LAND. WHERE THE MAIN TRACK SWINGS LEFT GO STRAIGHT ON - ONTO A SMALLER TRACK WHICH EVENTUALLY LEADS TO A GATE ONTO OPEN COMMONLAND. CONTINUE ALONG THE TRACK (THERE ARE A COUPLE OF PARALLEL ALTERNATIVES IN SOME PLACES - BUT BEWARE OF ANY THAT SWING AWAY TO THE RIGHT). SMOOTH GRASS RIDING BRINGS YOU ALONG TO MITCHELL'S FOLD STONE CIRCLE.

ACCORDING TO LEGEND THERE WAS ONCE A GREAT FAMINE IN THE REGION. THE DESPERATE PRAYERS OF THE LOCAL PEOPLE WERE FINALLY ANSWERED BY A FAIRY WHO GAVE THEM A MAGIC COW WITH AN ENDLESS SUPPLY OF MILK. BUT A WITCH CALLED MITCHELL TRIED TO MILK THE COW DRY. THE MAGIC COW VANISHED LEAVING MITCHELL ROOTED TO THE SPOT BY A SPELL - AND THE ANGRY LOCALS PENNED HER IN WITH A RING OF STONES.

CONTINUE ALONG THE GRASS TRACK TO THE EDGE OF THE COMMON AND THEN DOWN THE MUDDY LANE BACK TO THE START OF THE RIDE.

 The Devil's Chair at dusk. (Time to get away before the Demons come out to play!)

IRONBRIDGE TAKES ITS NAME FROM THE WORLD'S FIRST IRON BRIDGE BUILT ACROSS THE RIVER SEVERN IN 1779 BY ABRAHAM DARBY III. THE DARBY FAMILY OWNED THE IRON WORKS IN COALBROOKDALE AND THE BRIDGE WAS JUST ONE OF THEIR MANY IRON INNOVATIONS. PROBABLY THE MOST IMPORTANT WAS IN 1709 WHEN ABRAHAM DARBY I (THEY WERE INNOVATIVE WITH IRON – BUT NOT WITH NAMES!) EXPERIMENTED WITH A COKE (INSTEAD OF CHARCOAL) FUELLED BLAST FURNACE. THE PROCESS ENABLED LARGE QUANTITIES OF CHEAP, HIGH QUALITY IRON TO BE PRODUCED – PROVIDING THE ESSENTIAL MATERIAL FOR MAKING ALL THE ENGINES AND MACHINES THAT TRANSFORMED THE WORLD DURING THE INDUSTRIAL REVOLUTION.

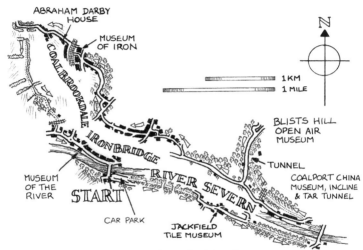

A TOWN THAT CLAIMS TO BE THE BIRTHPLACE OF THE INDUSTRIAL REVOLUTION PROBABLY DOESN'T SOUND LIKE AN IDEAL PLACE FOR A MOUNTAIN BIKE ROUTE. BUT YOU'LL FIND THAT IRONBRIDGE IS A SURPRISINGLY GREEN AND RURAL PLACE. THIS ISN'T ENTIRELY COINCIDENCE. THE WOODLANDS THAT CLOAK THE VALLEY SIDES WERE ONCE A VALUABLE SOURCE OF TIMBER FOR BUILDINGS, PIT PROPS, BOATS AND CHARCOAL (BEFORE THE FURNACES CONVERTED TO COKE). THE RIVER ITSELF WAS A VITAL TRANSPORT LINK – BUSTLING WITH BOATS FROM GLOUCESTER, WORCESTER AND BRISTOL IN THE DAYS BEFORE CANALS, RAILWAYS OR DECENT ROADS.

THIS EASY ROUTE IS IDEAL FOR NOVICE RIDERS. IT ALSO MAKES A BRILLIANT WAY TO TOUR THE FASCINATING IRONBRIDGE GORGE MUSEUMS. (AND YOU DON'T NEED TO WORRY ABOUT GETTING THIRSTY – I COUNTED 15 PUBS ON THIS ROUTE – OR THEREABOUTS – I LOST COUNT A BIT TOWARDS THE END!)

IRON BRIDGE

MAP: LANDRANGER 127, BUT PATHFINDER 890 IS MUCH MORE USEFUL
DISTANCE: 9½ MILES/15 KM   OFFROAD: 3½ MILES /5.5 KM
TIME: 1-2 HOURS
HIGHEST POINT: 515 FT / 155 M
TOTAL CLIMBING: 700 FT / 210 M
START: SOUTH END OF THE IRON BRIDGE (BESIDE THE OLD TOLL HOUSE) 672 034

FROM THE END OF THE IRON BRIDGE HEAD AWAY FROM THE RIVER AND, ALMOST
IMMEDIATELY TURN LEFT INTO A CAR PARK. AT THE FAR END, WHERE THE
CAR PARK EXIT ROAD BEARS RIGHT UP TO THE ROAD, GO STRAIGHT ON - ONTO A
TREE LINED TRACK. THIS IS THE ROUTE OF THE OLD SEVERN VALLEY RAILWAY
- NOW PART OF THE SEVERN VALLEY WAY. FOLLOW THIS TRACK FOR ¾ MILE (1KM)
UNTIL YOU EMERGE ONTO A ROAD BY SOME IMPRESSIVE OLD LEVEL CROSSING
GATES. TURN RIGHT AND THEN AFTER 300 YARDS LEFT (EFFECTIVELY STRAIGHT
ON). FOLLOW THIS ROAD PAST THE JACKFIELD TILE MUSEUM AND THEN ALONG
A BIZARRE SECTION OF ROAD SURFACED WITH PLANKS (AN ATTEMPT TO
OVERCOME SUBSIDENCE WHICH IS A MAJOR PROBLEM HERE). WHERE THE ROAD
TURNS SHARP LEFT GO STRAIGHT ON - BACK ONTO THE OLD RAILWAY LINE.
FOLLOW THIS FOR ½ MILE (0.8 KM) UNTIL THE TRACK IS BLOCKED AND YOU
DUCK DOWN A NARROW PATH TO THE LEFT (WATCH OUT FOR WALKERS), PAST
A PICNIC SITE AND UP SOME STEPS TO THE ROAD. TURN LEFT AND CROSS
COALPORT BRIDGE.

IMMEDIATELY OVER THE BRIDGE TURN LEFT THROUGH A GATE ONTO THE
SILKIN WAY - ANOTHER OLD RAILWAY (CHECK OUT THE WAGON WHEEL SIGNS).
PAST SOME COTTAGES YOU MEET A ROAD. TO VISIT THE COALPORT CLAY MUSEUM,
TAR TUNNEL AND HAY INCLINE TURN LEFT ALONG THIS ROAD. OTHERWISE CROSS
THE ROAD AND PICK UP THE TRACK AGAIN. THE ROUTE TAKES YOU UNDER
THE HAY INCLINE WHERE BOATS WERE LOWERED FROM THE CANAL ON THE
HILLTOP, DOWN TO COALPORT ON RAILWAY TROLLEYS. FURTHER ON YOU PASS
THROUGH A TUNNEL AND THEN EMERGE BESIDE A ROAD. TO VISIT BLIST'S
HILL OPEN AIR MUSEUM CONTINUE UP THE SILKIN WAY FOR ½ MILE (0.8KM).
OTHERWISE TURN LEFT DOWN THE ROAD.

TURN RIGHT TOWARDS IRONBRIDGE AT THE BOTTOM OF THE HILL. AFTER
¾ MILE (1KM) TURN RIGHT UP A LITTLE ROAD. FOLLOW THE ROAD UP, WIGGLING
PAST COTTAGES, TO A T-JUNCTION. TURN LEFT AND THEN RIGHT INTO BELMONT
ROAD. THIS AREA AT THE TOP OF IRON BRIDGE IS A PICTURESQUE CLUTTER
OF OLD MINE AND IRON WORKERS' COTTAGES. FOLLOW THE ROAD TO A
T-JUNCTION. TURN RIGHT, THEN LEFT AND LEFT AGAIN ONTO A ROAD THAT
DROPS DOWN INTO THE BACK OF COALBROOKDALE. CROSS THE MAIN

ROAD AT A JUNCTION AND DROP DOWN PAST THE COALBROOKDALE Co
IRONWORKS AND THE MUSEUM OF IRON. UNDER A BRIDGE BEAR RIGHT
ALONGSIDE THE RAILWAY VIADUCT, THEN LEFT UP THE HILL PAST ABRAHAM
DARBY'S HOUSE.

KEEP CLIMBING, THROUGH A WOOD AND PAST A HOUSING ESTATE AND
SOME COTTAGES. A LITTLE FURTHER ON THERE IS A SMALL PASSING PLACE ON
THE RIGHT WHERE THE ROAD STARTS TO FLATTEN OUT AT THE TOP OF THE HILL.
100 YARDS ON LOOK FOR AN OPENING IN THE HEDGE ON YOUR LEFT WITH A
SUPERB VIEW ACROSS THE VALLEY, DOMINATED BY THE HUGE POWER STATION
AT BUILDWAS. DROP DOWN THROUGH THE FIELD TO THE HEDGE CORNER
WHERE YOU'LL FIND A SMALL GATE. GO THROUGH AND DROP DOWN THROUGH
THE NEXT FIELDS, FOLLOWING THE HEDGE ON YOUR LEFT. 3/4 MILE (1KM)
OF FUN DOWNHILL BRINGS YOU TO A GATE INTO A SMALL WOOD. KEEP
THE FENCE ON YOUR LEFT STILL AND FOLLOW THE OBVIOUS PATH DOWN
ANOTHER FUN SECTION. GO THROUGH ANOTHER GATE AT THE BOTTOM
AND EMERGE ONTO A TRACK. THIS BECOMES TARMAC AS IT DROPS
DOWN TO A RAILWAY LEVEL CROSSING AND THEN TO THE ROAD. GO LEFT
AT THE JUNCTION AND THEN STRAIGHT ON AT A ROUNDABOUT AFTER
200 YARDS. CONTINUE PAST THE MUSEUM OF THE RIVER AND ALONG THE
RIVERSIDE ROAD BACK TO THE IRON BRIDGE. (PLEASE CROSS THE BRIDGE ON FOOT).

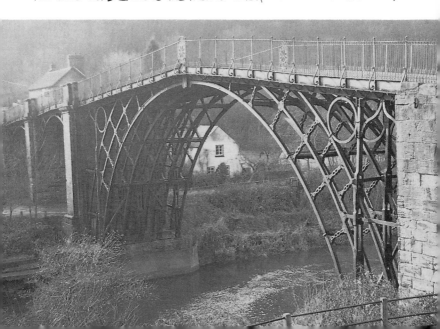

THINGS TO SEE - INDUSTRY

MOST OF MID-WALES AND THE MARCHES HAVE ESCAPED THE RAVAGES OF LARGE SCALE INDUSTRIAL DEVELOPMENT. BUT IN A FEW PLACES THE REMAINS OF OLD MILLS, MINES, FURNACES AND OTHER WORKS CAN BE FOUND LURKING BENEATH THE MOSS AND UNDERGROWTH.

MOST INDUSTRIES IN THE RURAL AREAS INVOLVED DIGGING HOLES IN THE GROUND. QUARRIES RANGED FROM A SMALL HOLE WHERE A FARMER MIGHT DIG OUT A FEW STONES TO BUILD A WALL, TO THE HUGE COMMERCIAL ENTERPRISES THAT HAVE RIPPED AWAY LARGE CHUNKS OF HILLSIDE SUCH AS AT CORRIS OR TITTERSTONE CLEE.

MINING WAS ANOTHER HOLE DIGGING INDUSTRY. GOLD HAS BEEN MINED IN WALES SINCE ROMAN TIMES AND OTHER VALUABLE MATERIALS, SUCH AS SILVER, LEAD, COPPER, IRON AND COAL HAVE ALSO BEEN WORKED OVER THE CENTURIES. EARLY MINES TENDED TO BE SMALL SCALE AFFAIRS - JUST A FEW PEOPLE DIGGING SHALLOW SHAFTS WITH HORSES OPERATING THE WINDING GEAR AND MACHINERY. (IN A FEW PLACES SMALL SCALE MINING CONTINUED INTO THE 20TH CENTURY - SOMETIMES USING AN UPTURNED BICYCLE FOR THE MINE HEAD GEAR!) LARGER MINES APPEARED DURING THE INDUSTRIAL REVOLUTION. LEAD MINING WAS AN IMPORTANT INDUSTRY AROUND THE STIPERSTONES. COAL AND IRON ORE WERE EXTRACTED ON A LARGE SCALE AROUND IRONBRIDGE, PROVIDING FUEL AND RAW MATERIAL FOR THE NUMEROUS LOCAL IRON FOUNDRIES.

IN THE EARLY DAYS PRODUCTS AND MATERIALS WERE TRANSPORTED BY HORSE-DRAWN WAGGONS OR PACK HORSES, OR BY BOAT AROUND THE COAST AND ALONG THE LARGER RIVERS. WITH THE BOOM IN PRODUCTION DURING THE INDUSTRIAL REVOLUTION THERE CAME A NEED FOR BETTER TRANSPORT, BUT THE NEW CANALS AND RAILWAYS WERE DIFFICULT TO BUILD IN HILLY TERRAIN. CANAL BUILDERS TRIED INGENIOUS IDEAS SUCH AS THE INCLINES NEAR IRONBRIDGE WHERE BOATS WERE RAISED FROM ONE LEVEL TO ANOTHER ON RAILWAY TROLLEYS, OR THE HUGE AQUEDUCT ACROSS THE VALLEY AT PONTCYSYLLTE NEAR LLANGOLLEN. NARROW GAUGE RAILWAYS WERE CHEAPER AND EASIER TO BUILD THAN FULL SIZE LINES AND WERE USED TO SERVE A NUMBER OF INDUSTRIES, SUCH AS THOSE AT CORRIS AND THE STIPERSTONES.

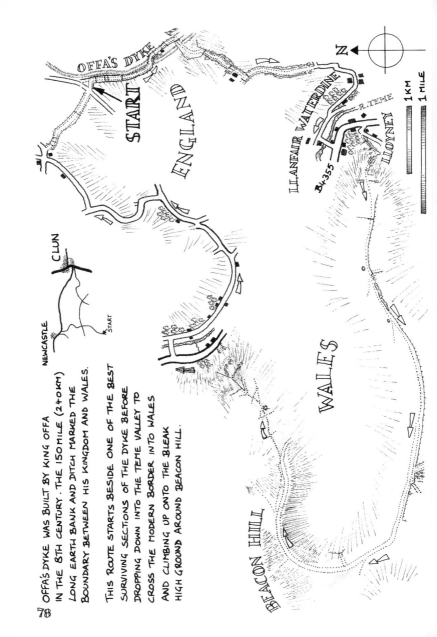

OFFA'S DYKE WAS BUILT BY KING OFFA
IN THE 8TH CENTURY. THE 150 MILE (240 KM)
LONG EARTH BANK AND DITCH MARKED THE
BOUNDARY BETWEEN HIS KINGDOM AND WALES.

THIS ROUTE STARTS BESIDE ONE OF THE BEST
SURVIVING SECTIONS OF THE DYKE BEFORE
DROPPING DOWN INTO THE TEME VALLEY TO
CROSS THE MODERN BORDER INTO WALES
AND CLIMBING UP ONTO THE BLEAK
HIGH GROUND AROUND BEACON HILL.

OFFA'S DYKE

START

ENGLAND

N

LLANFAIR WATERDINE

R. TEME

LLOYNEY

B4-355

1 KM

1 MILE

WALES

BEACON HILL

CLUN

NEWCASTLE

START

BEACON HILL & OFFA'S DYKE ROUTE 13

MAP: LANDRANGERS 136 + 137. MOST OF THE ROUTE IS ALSO ON LANDRANGER 148 AND PATHFINDERS 949 + 950
DISTANCE: 19 MILES / 30 KM   OFFROAD: 12½ MILES / 19.5 KM
TIME: 2½ - 4 HOURS
HIGHEST POINT: 1670 FT / 510 M
TOTAL CLIMBING: 2300 FT / 700 M
START: END OF TRACK BY OFFA'S DYKE 249 797

PARK ON THE GRASS VERGE BY THE START OF THE TRACK. THERE'S
ROOM FOR A COUPLE OF CARS, BUT MAKE SURE YOU DON'T BLOCK THE ROAD,
TRACK OR GATES. ALTERNATIVELY YOU COULD TAKE THE TRAIN TO KNUCKLAS
ON THE SCENIC CENTRAL WALES LINE - ONLY A MILE AND A HALF (2.5 KM)
DOWN THE VALLEY FROM LLOYNEY (CHECK THE TRAIN TIMES FIRST - THEY'RE
A BIT IRREGULAR).

SET OFF ALONG THE CLEAR TRACK THAT HEADS SOUTH ALONGSIDE
OFFA'S DYKE. (DON'T BE TEMPTED TO RIDE ALONG THE TOP OF THE DYKE - ITS A
FOOTPATH ONLY.) AFTER A MILE (1.5 KM), AND VARIOUS GATES, THE TRACK
SWINGS LEFT THROUGH A GAP IN THE ANCIENT EARTHWORK. PASS A PATCH OF
SMALL TREES AND A BARN, AND THEN BY SOME OLD WINDSWEPT SCOTS PINES
TURN RIGHT THROUGH A GATE. FOLLOW THE TRACK THROUGH ANOTHER
GAP IN THE DYKE AND DOWN THE HILL ON A FAST (BUT IN PLACES ROUGH)
DESCENT.

AFTER 3/4 MILE (1 KM) YOU PASS A BARN (PICK YOUR LINE CAREFULLY
IF YOU DON'T WANT TO END UP HUB-DEEP IN SOMETHING UNPLEASANT !!).
TURN LEFT AFTER THE BARN AND CONTINUE DOWN THE TRACK. GO
STRAIGHT ON WHEN THE TRACK FINALLY MEETS A TINY ROAD AND
FOLLOW THE TARMAC DOWN THROUGH A FARMYARD AND WOOD TO A
JUNCTION. TURN RIGHT (EFFECTIVELY STRAIGHT ON) AND THEN AFTER
300 YARDS SWING LEFT TO CROSS THE RIVER TEME AND THE MODERN
BOUNDARY INTO WALES.

AT THE T-JUNCTION TURN LEFT ONTO THE B4355. AFTER 200 YARDS
TURN RIGHT UP A STEEP LITTLE ROAD, THEN AFTER PASSING A COTTAGE ON
EITHER SIDE TURN RIGHT UP A STEEP TRACK INTO A DARK OLD WOOD. IT'S
ONLY A SHORT HAUL TO THE GATE AT THE END OF THE WOOD - BUT
WORTH EXTRA EGO POINTS IF YOU MANAGE TO RIDE IT ALL THE WAY!
BEYOND THE GATE CONTINUE ALONGSIDE THE HEDGE AT THE BOTTOM
OF AN OVERGROWN FIELD. GO THROUGH ANOTHER GATE AND THEN AT
THE END OF THE NEXT FIELD TURN RIGHT AND FOLLOW THE HEDGE
STRAIGHT UP THE HILL. HALFWAY UP IT GETS EVEN STEEPER AND THE

NARROW TRACK IS LINED WITH GORSE. (EARN YOURSELF A SHED FULL OF EGO POINTS IF YOU MANAGE TO MAKE IT TO THE TOP OF THE SLOPE WITHOUT STOPPING, GETTING OFF AND WALKING OR JUST COLLAPSING!) FOLLOW THE HEDGE UNTIL IT SWINGS AWAY TO THE LEFT AND CONTINUE STRAIGHT UP THE HILL TOWARDS A GAP IN A FENCE. BEYOND THE GAP BEAR LEFT ON A FAINT TRACK THAT SHORTLY REACHES ANOTHER FENCE ON YOUR LEFT.

THE NEXT 3 MILES (5 KM) ARE EASY. YOU SIMPLY FOLLOW THE FENCE ALONG THE TOP OF THE MOORLAND, GRADUALLY GAINING ALTITUDE AND WITH THE TRACK BECOMING MORE DEFINED THE FURTHER YOU GO. EVENTUALLY THE FENCE ENDS AND THE TRACK SWINGS RIGHT TOWARDS THE MAIN MASS OF BEACON HILL. FOLLOW THE MAIN TRACK AS IT DIPS DOWN THROUGH A FEW TWISTS, RUTS AND PUDDLEY SECTIONS AND THEN CLIMBS UP ACROSS THE RIGHT FLANK OF THE HILL. BEYOND THE HIGHEST POINT OF THE HILL, THE TRACK DROPS A LITTLE THEN RISES SLIGHTLY. KEEP TO THE MAIN TRACK, ON THE RIGHT, BUT LOOK OUT HERE FOR ANOTHER PARALLEL TRACK ON THE LEFT. AS THE GROUND LEVELS OFF AND THEN STARTS TO DESCEND LOOK OUT FOR WHERE THE PARALLEL TRACK REJOINS THE MAIN TRACK AND THEN A FEW YARDS FURTHER ON BEAR LEFT ON A FAINT NARROW TRACK. (BE CAREFUL HERE — THERE AREN'T MANY LANDMARKS AND IT'S EASY TO MISS THE TURN AS THE MAIN TRACK BECOMES A FAST DESCENT. IF YOU FIND YOURSELF SWINGING AWAY TO THE RIGHT AND BLASTING DOWN TOWARDS A GATE — YOU'VE MISSED THE TURN!)

FOLLOW THE NARROW TRACK AS IT GENTLY DESCENDS, GRADUALLY BECOMING MORE CLEARLY DEFINED AND FAST. GO STRAIGHT ACROSS AT A COUPLE OF TRACK JUNCTIONS, THEN SHORTLY AFTER PASSING A SMALL TREE ON YOUR RIGHT, BEAR LEFT ON A TRACK WHICH SHOULD TAKE YOU TO A FENCE AT THE POINTED TOP OF A FIELD. CLIMB OVER THE CORNER OF THE FENCE (OR GO THROUGH A NEW GATE WHEN ITS BUILT) INTO THE FIELD ON THE RIGHT. DROP DIAGONALLY DOWN THE SLOPE, THROUGH A GATE AND THEN STRAIGHT DOWN THE NEXT FIELD. PASS BETWEEN SOME TREES AND THEN YOU PICK UP AN OBVIOUS TRACK LEADING DOWN TO THE ROAD.

TURN LEFT ON THE ROAD AND CRUISE UP THE VALLEY. AFTER 1/3 MILE (0.5 KM) TURN RIGHT, CROSS THE BRIDGE BACK INTO ENGLAND AND THEN TURN RIGHT AGAIN. AFTER A MILE (1.5 KM) BEAR LEFT AND CONTINUE ALONG THE ROAD FOR ANOTHER MILE (1.5 KM) THEN BEAR LEFT AGAIN. A MILE AND A HALF (2.5 KM) OF STEADY UPHILL SLOG TAKES YOU BACK UP ONTO THE HILLTOPS. WHEN YOU REACH A JUNCTION TURN RIGHT AND CONTINUE UNTIL YOU REACH A CROSSROADS. TURN RIGHT AND THEN ALMOST IMMEDIATELY RIGHT AGAIN ONTO THE FINAL 3/4 MILE (1 KM) OF CLEAR, FAST TRACK BACK TO THE START.

THINGS TO SEE ~ GEOLOGY

THE CHANCES ARE THE ONLY TIME YOU THINK ABOUT GEOLOGY WHEN YOU'RE RIDING YOUR BIKE, IS WHEN YOU'RE TRYING TO DODGE NASTY LOOKING LUMPS OF IT STICKING OUT OF THE TRACK. BUT THERE'S MORE TO ROCKS THAN BUCKLED RIMS AND CHIPPED PAINT. GEOLOGY INFLUENCES THE WHOLE OF THE LANDSCAPE INCLUDING THE WILDLIFE, AGRICULTURE, INDUSTRY AND COMMUNITIES THAT YOU'LL FIND THERE. EVEN THINGS LIKE LOCAL STYLES OF ARCHITECTURE ARE AFFECTED BY THE TYPES OF STONE AVAILABLE FOR BUILDING MATERIALS. AND, OF COURSE, GEOLOGY ALSO DICTATES THE SIZE AND SHAPE OF THE HILLS.

WATCHING HILLS FORM IS NOT REALLY AN IDEAL HOBBY - UNLESS YOU'VE GOT A FEW HUNDRED MILLION YEARS TO SPARE! THE PROCESSES INVOLVED TEND TO BE UNIMAGINABLY SLOW, BUT THEY ARE ALSO PRETTY AWESOME.

THE SURFACE OF THE EARTH IS A JIGSAW OF DIFFERENT PLATES OF HARD ROCK, FLOATING ON TOP OF THE MOLTEN MAGMA BENEATH. THESE ARE ALL VERY SLOWLY MOVING. THE ROCKS THAT WE NOW FIND IN MID-WALES WERE FORMED IN A TROPICAL SEA THOUSANDS OF MILES SOUTH OF THEIR PRESENT LOCATION. MUD, SAND AND DEAD SEA CREATURES WERE DEPOSITED IN LAYERS ON THE SEA BED. AS MORE LAYERS BUILT UP ON TOP THE UNDERLYING SEDIMENTS WERE COMPRESSED AND FORMED HARD ROCK. OVER A PERIOD OF HUNDREDS OF MILLIONS OF YEARS THEY MOVED NORTHWARDS TOWARDS THEIR PRESENT LOCATION. IN THE PROCESS THEY BECAME SQUEEZED BETWEEN OTHER PLATES AND THE ROCKS BUCKLED UPWARDS TO FORM HUGE MOUNTAINS LIKE THE HIMALAYAS AND THE ALPS.

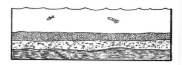

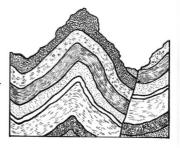

GRADUALLY THE MOUNTAINS WERE ERODED BY THE ELEMENTS. SOME OF THE MOST DRAMATIC EROSION CAME IN THE ICE AGES DURING THE LAST MILLION YEARS OR SO. IN NORTH WALES GLACIERS CARVED STEEP SIDED VALLEYS AND RIPPED HUGE HOLLOWS OUT OF THE SIDES OF MOUNTAINS SUCH AS CADAIR IDRIS. THE SOFTER ROCKS OF MID WALES ALLOWED A CONTINUOUS ICE SHEET TO SLIDE ACROSS THE WHOLE LANDSCAPE, SCULPTING THE ROUNDED HILLS WE FIND TODAY.

THINGS TO SEE – HILL FARMING

WELSH HILL FARMING TODAY CAN BE SUMMARISED IN ONE WORD – SHEEP! YOU'LL FIND THEM EVERYWHERE FROM COASTAL SAND DUNES TO THE SUMMITS OF THE HIGHEST MOUNTAINS. THE TRADITIONAL METHOD OF FARMING THE WELSH HILLS WAS THE HAFOD/HENDRE SYSTEM. DURING THE WINTER SHORT, STOCKY WELSH MOUNTAIN CATTLE WERE KEPT AT THE HENDRE – THE MAIN LOWLAND FARM. ON MAYDAY THEY WERE MOVED UP TO THE HAFOD – A SUMMER GRAZING FARM IN THE HILLS – AND THE HENDRE FIELDS WERE USED FOR GROWING CROPS. GRADUALLY FARMERS TRIED TO MAKE USE OF LAND HIGHER AND HIGHER UP THE HILLS. MANY CHANGED FROM CATTLE TO SHEEP, AS THEY WERE BETTER ADAPTED TO POOR GRASSLAND AND EXPOSED CONDITIONS. ACCORDING TO CUSTOM IF A FARMER BUILT A HUT ON OPEN MOORLAND AND HAD A FIRE BURNING IN THE HEARTH BEFORE NIGHTFALL HE COULD KEEP HIS ANIMALS ON THE LAND WITHIN THE DISTANCE OF AN AXE THROW FROM IT. (OR MAYBE THE FARMERS JUST FOUND THAT IF THEY STARTED THROWING AXES AROUND PEOPLE LET THEM HAVE THE LAND!)

FARMING THE HILLS HAS NEVER BEEN EASY AND TODAY MANY SMALL UPLAND FARMS HAVE BEEN ABANDONED. SHEEP STILL GRAZE MANY HILLS, BUT WITH MOTORBIKES AND FOUR WHEEL DRIVE VEHICLES GIVING EASY ACCESS TO THE HIGH GROUND FARMERS NO LONGER HAVE TO SPEND THE SUMMER LIVING IN A HAFOD.

MOST OF THE ANIMALS FROM WELSH FARMS WERE NOT CONSUMED LOCALLY, BUT WENT TO FEED PEOPLE IN LONDON AND THE MIDLANDS. IN THE DAYS BEFORE LORRIES OR TRAINS THE ONLY WAY TO GET ANIMALS TO THE DISTANT MARKETS WAS TO MAKE THEM WALK. FARMERS ENTRUSTED THEIR CATTLE, PIGS, SHEEP AND EVEN GEESE TO DROVERS WHO WOULD MARCH HUGE HERDS HUNDREDS OF MILES, OVER THE WELSH MOUNTAINS AND ACROSS ENGLAND. A TYPICAL JOURNEY WOULD TAKE 2-3 WEEKS. RETURNING WAS QUICKER – BUT ALSO MORE DANGEROUS AS THE DROVERS CARRIED THE PROFITS FROM SELLING THE ANIMALS AND WERE OFTEN ATTACKED BY BANDITS.

ALTHOUGH DROVING HAS LONG SINCE DIED OUT, IT HAS LEFT TWO NOTEABLE LEGACIES: – CORGI DOGS WERE SPECIALLY BRED FOR DROVING. THEIR SMALL SIZE ALLOWED THEM TO RUN BETWEEN THE LEGS OF CATTLE.
– DROVE ROADS WERE SPECIAL ROUTES FOR LIVESTOCK ACROSS THE HILLS. MANY SURVIVE AS GREEN LANES AND ARE EXCELLENT FOR MOUNTAIN BIKING.

TO BE HONEST TITTERSTONE CLEE IS NOT A PRETTY PLACE. CENTURIES OF QUARRYING
HAVE RIPPED HUGE HOLES OUT OF THE HILL, SCATTERED SPOIL TIPS DOWN THE SLOPES
AND LEFT A NETWORK OF SHATTERED, DERELICT ROADS THAT GIVE IT THE
FEELING OF A POST-APOCALYPSE LANDSCAPE IN SOME PLACES.

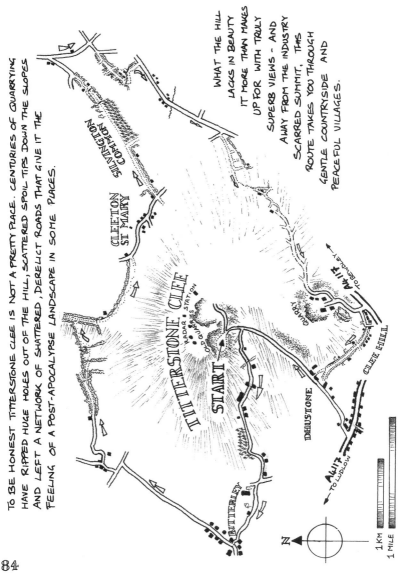

WHAT THE HILL
LACKS IN BEAUTY
IT MORE THAN MAKES
UP FOR WITH TRULY
SUPERB VIEWS - AND
AWAY FROM THE INDUSTRY
SCARRED SUMMIT, THIS
ROUTE TAKES YOU THROUGH
GENTLE COUNTRYSIDE AND
PEACEFUL VILLAGES.

SILVINGTON COMMON

CLEETON ST MARY

TITTERSTONE CLEE

RADAR STATION
OLD QUARRIES

START

QUARRY

A4117 TO GENEVA

CLEE HILL

DHUSTONE

A4117 TO LUDLOW

BITTERLEY

N

1 KM
1 MILE

TITTERSTONE CLEE

MAP: LANDRANGER 138 OR PATH FINDERS 951 AND 952
DISTANCE: 17 MILES /27 KM   OFFROAD: 5½ MILES /9 KM
TIME: 1½ – 2½ HOURS
HIGHEST POINT: 1600FT /490M
TOTAL CLIMBING: 1800FT /550M
START: CAR PARK IN TITTERSTONE CLEE QUARRY   593 777

START FROM THE CAR PARK IN THE OLD QUARRY (UP THE ROAD SIGNED
TO DHUSTONE OFF THE A4117). THE RUINED WORKINGS ARE OF
INTEREST TO INDUSTRIAL HISTORY ENTHUSIASTS (WHILE THE
SURROUNDING SPOIL TIPS ARE A FEARSOME UNOFFICIAL PLAYGROUND
FOR MOTOCROSSERS). QUARRYING ISN'T THE ONLY ACTIVITY TO HAVE
RESHAPED THE HILL. IRON AGE PEOPLE BUILT A HILLFORT ON THE SUMMIT OVER
2000 YEARS AGO AND IN LATER TIMES THERE WERE COALMINES, IRON
FURNACES, GLASSWORKS AND LIME KILNS ON THE SURROUNDING SLOPES.
TODAY THE SUMMIT IS CROWNED WITH THE CIVIL AVIATION AUTHORITY'S
RADAR STATION. ON A CLEAR DAY THE VIEW FROM THE START OF THE RIDE
IS BRILLIANT - ACROSS LUDLOW AND SOUTH SHROPSHIRE TO THE DISTANT
MOUNTAINS OF WALES, FROM SNOWDONIA IN THE NORTH TO THE BRECON
BEACONS IN THE SOUTH.

FROM THE CAR PARK DROP BACK DOWN THE ROAD FOR ABOUT 400 YARDS AND
TURN RIGHT ONTO A VERY SMALL ROAD. VERY ROUGH IN PLACES, THIS DROPS DOWN
TO A GATE AT THE EDGE OF THE OPEN MOORLAND. BEYOND THE GATE IT'S A SMOOTH
TARMAC DESCENT FOR 1⅓ MILES (2KM) TO A T-JUNCTION. TURN RIGHT
-EFFECTIVELY GOING STRAIGHT ON (NOT DOWN THE NO-THROUGH ROAD TO BITTERLEY
CHURCH-UNLESS YOU'RE INTO ECCLESIASTICAL ARCHITECTURE AND WANT TO SEE
THE HALF-TIMBERED SPIRE). ANOTHER ¾ MILE (1KM) BRINGS YOU INTO
BITTERLEY VILLAGE WHERE YOU SHOULD TURN RIGHT OPPOSITE THE LITTLE SCHOOL.

FOLLOW THE ROAD FOR 1¼ MILES (2KM) AND THEN TURN RIGHT SHORTLY AFTER A
SHARP LEFT BEND. TAKE THE NEXT TURN ON THE RIGHT AND RIDE UP A SMALL ROAD
WHICH EVENTUALLY TURNS INTO A GOOD HEDGED TRACK. WHERE THE TRACK FORKS
- ONE BRANCH GOING LEFT INTO A FIELD AND THE OTHER RIGHT BETWEEN HIGH
HEDGES - BEAR RIGHT. GO THROUGH A GATE AND STRAIGHT ON ALONG THE EDGE OF
A FIELD. THROUGH ANOTHER GATE AND CROSS THE NEXT FIELD TO A 3RD GATE.
BEYOND THIS GATE TURN LEFT BESIDE A SMALL WOOD THEN RIGHT AND FOLLOW
THE HEDGE UP THE FIELD. AT THE TOP OF THE FIELD GO THROUGH ANOTHER
GATE AND TURN RIGHT ALONG A HEDGED GREEN LANE. THIS LANE GETS A BIT
OVERGROWN IN PLACES - LEAVING A NARROW PATH UP THE MIDDLE (WATCH OUT -
THERE ARE A FEW WICKED LITTLE ROCKS WHICH SNEAK UNDER YOUR WHEELS AND

TRY TO TIP YOU INTO THE UNDERGROWTH). GO THROUGH THE GATE AT THE END OF THE LANE AND BEAR LEFT, PAST A FARMHOUSE, FOLLOWING THE HEDGE ALONG THE EDGE OF THE MOORLAND. 1 MILE (1.5 KM) OF WIGGLY SHEEPTRACK FUN EVENTUALLY BRINGS YOU TO THE ROAD.

TURN RIGHT TO CLEETON ST MARY. BEYOND THE VILLAGE CONTINUE FOR 300 YARDS THEN SWING LEFT ONTO A WIDE, FAST TRACK LEADING ONTO SILVINGTON COMMON. WHERE THE MAIN TRACK SWINGS RIGHT BY THE CORNER OF A FOREST GO STRAIGHT ON ONTO SMOOTH GRASS. CRUISE ALONG UNTIL YOU REACH A GATE. GO THROUGH AND CONTINUE STRAIGHT ON, PAST A FARM AND DOWN THE GRAVEL TRACK TO THE ROAD. GO STRAIGHT ON AND FOLLOW THE TARMAC TO A T-JUNCTION. TURN RIGHT AND WHEN YOU REACH A CROSSROADS GO RIGHT AGAIN. WHERE THE ROAD BENDS LEFT GO STRAIGHT ON UP A WIDE TRACK. IGNORE TRACKS OFF TO EITHER SIDE AND CONTINUE UNTIL YOU REACH A GATE LEADING OUT ONTO OPEN MOORLAND. GO THROUGH AND FOLLOW THE TRACK DOWN TO THE ROAD.

TURN RIGHT ON THE TARMAC AND ZOOM ALONG FOR 1 MILE (1.5 KM) UNTIL YOU MEET A ROAD ON YOUR RIGHT. TURN RIGHT AND THEN IMMEDIATELY LEFT ONTO A GRAVEL TRACK WHICH CLIMBS GENTLY UP THE HILL. WHERE THE GRAVEL FINALLY SWINGS OFF TO THE LEFT CONTINUE UP THE GRASSY SLOPE ON A PATH WHICH CURVES GENTLY LEFT TO SOME OLD MINER'S COTTAGES. YOU ROLL ONTO GRAVEL AGAIN AS YOU PASS BETWEEN THE HOUSES AND CONTINUE THE STEADY CLIMB. GO STRAIGHT ON WHERE A FORK SWINGS UP TO SOME HOUSES ON THE RIGHT AND CONTINUE TO A SEMI-DERELICT ROAD AND BEAR LEFT. AMAZING VIEWS STRETCH OUT TO THE SOUTH AND EAST, OVER THE ROLLING HILLS OF HEREFORDSHIRE TO THE MALVERNS AND THE DISTANT COTSWOLDS. AFTER A MILE (1.5 KM) OF POTHOLE SLALOM YOU DROP DOWN PAST MODERN QUARRY WORKINGS. BEWARE OF LORRIES AND HEAVY MACHINERY AND OBSERVE THE 15 MPH (24 KPH) SPEED LIMIT. (ITS NOT OFTEN THAT CYCLISTS HAVE TO WORRY ABOUT KEEPING TO THE SPEED LIMIT ON THE ROAD!) PASS AN OLD FLOODED QUARRY AND THEN JUST BEFORE MEETING THE MAIN ROAD TURN RIGHT ONTO A SMOOTH TRACK PAST THE CLEE HILL PLANT HIRE DEPOT. AFTER A SHARP LEFT HAND BEND TURN RIGHT, THROUGH A GATE ONTO THE ROUTE OF AN OLD MINERAL RAILWAY. (PLEASE NOTE – ALTHOUGH ITS WELL USED THE OLD RAILWAY TRACKBED IS NOT A PUBLIC RIGHT OF WAY. IF YOU ENCOUNTER PROBLEMS – LEAVE THE ROUTE AND CHECK THE O.S. MAP FOR AN ALTERNATIVE WAY ROUND). ZIP ALONG THE TRACK FOR 3/4 MILE (1 KM) UNTIL ANOTHER GATE LEADS YOU OUT BETWEEN SOME HOUSES TO THE ROAD. FROM HERE WAGONS LOADED WITH STONE FROM THE QUARRIES WERE WINCHED DOWN A STEEP INCLINE TO THE MAIN RAILWAY LINE 600FT (180M) BELOW. TURN RIGHT AND ITS 1¼ MILES (2 KM) OF GENTLE TARMAC CLIMBING BACK TO THE START.

THE RIVER RHEIDOL HAS CARVED AN IMPRESSIVELY DEEP VALLEY ON ITS WAY DOWN TO THE SEA AT ABERYSTWYTH. TUMBLING STREAMS PLUNGE DOWN OVER SPECTACULAR WATERFALLS BEFORE JOINING THE MAIN RIVER, AND THE STEEP VALLEY SIDES ARE CLOAKED WITH ANCIENT OAK WOODLAND – MUCH OF WHICH IS NOW PROTECTED AS A NATIONAL NATURE RESERVE.

DEVIL'S BRIDGE & THE VALE OF RHEIDOL ROU

MAP: LANDRANGER 135 OR PATHFINDER 947
DISTANCE: 14½ MILES / 23 KM   OFFROAD: 4½ MILES / 7 KM
TIME: 2–3½ HOURS
HIGHEST POINT: 1230 FT / 375 M
TOTAL CLIMBING: 1800 FT / 550 M
START: LAYBY + PICNIC AREA BESIDE CWM RHEIDOL RESERVOIR   695 796

HEAD DOWN THE VALLEY FOR 350 YARDS AND TURN LEFT. THE ROAD CROSSES A BRIDGE AND THEN TURNS RIGHT. AFTER 400 YARDS LOOK FOR A BRIDLEWAY SIGN ON THE LEFT. GO THROUGH THE GATE AND CLIMB STEEPLY TO ANOTHER GATE. CROSS THE RAILWAY AND GO INTO THE FOREST BEYOND. FOLLOW THE TRACK UNTIL YOU EMERGE FROM THE TREES AND THEN BEAR LEFT. CROSS ANOTHER TRACK, BEARING LEFT A LITTLE FURTHER ON, AND THEN RIGHT. NEAR THE TOP OF THE WOOD SWING LEFT UP A PATH TO A GATE. GO STRAIGHT ACROSS THE FIELD TO THE RIGHT-HAND END OF THE TRACK YOU CAN SEE CARVED ACROSS A TREE COVERED RISE. FOLLOW THE TRACK THROUGH A GATE, PAST AN ABANDONED FARM AND ALONG TO THE ROAD. TURN LEFT, CLIMB UP TO A T-JUNCTION AND GO LEFT AGAIN. CRUISE ALONG FOR 3 MILES (5 KM) TO DEVIL'S BRIDGE, ADMIRING THE VIEWS DOWN INTO THE VALLEY AND ACROSS TO THE RHEIDOL FALLS.

TO SEE THE BRIDGES AND WATERFALLS AT DEVIL'S BRIDGE YOU'LL NEED TO LOCK UP YOUR BIKE AND PAY TO WALK DOWN INTO THE GORGE. AFTERWARDS RIDE BACK TO THE JUNCTION JUST BEFORE THE BRIDGE AND TURN UP THE B4574, WITH

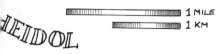

THE DEVIL'S BRIDGE IS ACTUALLY THREE BRIDGES - ONE ON TOP OF THE OTHER. THE ORIGINAL SPAN WAS BUILT BY MONKS IN 1188 AND THE OTHERS ADDED IN 1753 AND 1901. FOR NEARLY A CENTURY THE TINY STEAM TRAINS ON THE VALE OF RHEIDOL RAILWAY HAVE BEEN BRINGING PASSENGERS TO SEE THE BRIDGES AND THE DRAMATIC WATERFALLS NEARBY.

THIS ROUTE COMBINES THE MOST SCENIC PARTS OF THE VALLEY WITH SOME OF THE BEST RIDING IN THE AREA.

THE OLD AA BOX ON THE CORNER. AFTER 2 MILES (3KM) OF GENTLE CLIMBING LOOK FOR SIGNS FOR A FOREST PICNIC AREA, THEN OPPOSITE A TOILET BUILDING TURN RIGHT THROUGH A GATE ONTO AN EXCELLENT TRACK. IGNORE A STEEP TRACK UP TO THE LEFT AND FOLLOW THE GENTLY DESCENDING TRACK THROUGH A COUPLE OF GATES TO THE CORNER OF A FOREST. FORK RIGHT ALONG THE EDGE OF THE WOOD ON A GRASSY TRACK THAT TAKES YOU THROUGH THE FOREST AND OUT THROUGH FIELDS DROPPING DOWN TO THE ROAD BY A COTTAGE.

TURN RIGHT ON THE ROAD, THEN LEFT AFTER 100 YARDS. LEFT AT THE NEXT JUNCTION AND THEN RIGHT. TURN LEFT WHEN YOU REACH THE MAIN ROAD, THEN AFTER ⅓ MILE (0.5KM) TURN RIGHT DOWN THE BRIDLEWAY TO TY'N-Y-CASTELL FARM. UP INTO THE FARMYARD TURN RIGHT, PAST THE HOUSE AND TO A GATE. THROUGH THE GATE RIDE TO ANOTHER GATE BUT DON'T GO THROUGH - CONTINUE ALONGSIDE THE HEDGE UNTIL YOU EMERGE INTO ANOTHER FIELD. CROSS THE FIELD, BEARING SLIGHTLY RIGHT TO A GATE INTO THE WOOD. DON'T GO THROUGH THE GATE, BUT TURN RIGHT AND FOLLOW THE FENCE TO A CORNER. CLIMB OVER THE FENCE (OR GO THROUGH THE GATE IF ITS BEEN BUILT). TURN LEFT AND FOLLOW A SUNKEN TRACK DOWN BETWEEN THE TREES. AFTER ABOUT 100 YARDS THE TRACK SWINGS LEFT THROUGH A GATE AND CONTINUES DOWNWARDS. BEWARE THERE ARE SOME STEEP AND

SLIPPY BITS DOWN HERE. (THE WOODED HILLSIDE IS A NATIONAL NATURE RESERVE SO PLEASE TREAT IT WITH RESPECT.)

WHEN YOU REACH THE RAILWAY LINE GO STRAIGHT ACROSS. (THE PATCH OF GRASS AND SIGN JUST DOWN THE TRACK ON YOUR LEFT ARE ACTUALLY A STATION!) CONTINUE DOWN THE STEEP TRACK WITH A FEW CLEARINGS ON THE RIGHT GIVING VIEWS ACROSS THE VALLEY. (THE RUSTY SCREES ARE THE REMAINS OF AN OLD LEAD AND ZINC MINE.) AT THE FENCE AT THE BOTTOM OF THE WOOD TURN SHARP RIGHT OFF THE MAIN TRACK TO A GATE INTO A FIELD. FOLLOW THE HEDGE TO A GOOD TRACK THAT DROPS DOWN PAST A HOUSE TO A WIDE, BUT RIDEABLE, FORD. (LOOK OUT FOR THE WACKY SCULPTURES ON AN ISLAND ON THE RIGHT). WHEN YOU REACH THE ROAD TURN LEFT AND CRUISE DOWN THE VALLEY FOR 2½ MILES (4KM), PAST THE HYDRO-ELECTRIC POWER STATION, AND BACK TO THE START.

▼ Satanic civil engineering at Devil's Bridge!

THINGS TO SEE ~ LEGENDS & SUPERSTITIONS

THE WILD COUNTRY OF MID-WALES AND THE MARCHES ABOUNDS WITH SPOOKY TALES OF EERIE AND SUPERNATURAL GOINGS ON.

CYNON WAS AN EVIL SPIRIT WHO LIVED IN THE LLANWDDYN VALLEY BEFORE IT WAS FLOODED TO CREATE LAKE VYRNWY. HE WAS CAUGHT BY A SORCERER WHO BURIED HIM BENEATH A HUGE BOULDER. AS LONG AS HE WAS IMPRISONED THERE THE PEOPLE OF THE VALLEY WERE SAFE - BUT THE BOULDER WAS MOVED DURING THE CONSTRUCTION OF THE DAM!

LLANGOLLEN'S NAME MEANS 'THE CHURCH OF ST COLLEN'. COLLEN WAS PROCLAIMED A SAINT AFTER HE KILLED A DEMON WHO HAD DISGUISED HIMSELF AS A FAIRY KING AND LURED COLLEN TO HIS MAGIC CASTLE.

THE REAL CASTLE AT LLANGOLLEN, CASTELL DINAS BRAN, FEATURES IN MANY LEGENDS AND IS SAID TO BE THE CASTLE OF THE HOLY GRAIL FROM THE TALES OF KING ARTHUR.

CADAIR IDRIS MEANS 'KING ARTHUR'S CHAIR', BUT IF YOU SIT DOWN TO REST ON THE MOUNTAIN TAKE CARE NOT TO FALL ASLEEP - OR YOU'LL WAKE UP MAD, BLIND OR A POET! AND IF THE 1000FT (300M) DROP FROM THE SUMMIT DOWN TO LLYN CAU DOESN'T FRIGHTEN YOU THEN PERHAPS THE TALES OF THE MAN-EATING MONSTER THAT LIVES IN THE LAKE WILL.

THE FIRST OF THE BRIDGES AT DEVIL'S BRIDGE IS SAID TO BE THE WORK OF THE DEVIL HIMSELF. HE BUILT IT FOR AN OLD WOMAN IN RETURN FOR THE SOUL OF THE FIRST LIVING THING TO CROSS IT. THE EVIL ONE HOPED TO CATCH THE WOMAN'S SON BUT SHE MADE HER DOG CROSS FIRST AND SATAN HAD TO RETURN TO HELL WITH ONLY A NEW PET FOR A PRIZE.

THERE ARE HUNDREDS OF OTHER TALES FEATURING DEMONS, GHOSTS, PHANTOM FUNERALS, WITCHES, FAIRIES, GOBLINS, VAMPIRES, GWRACH-Y-RHIBYN (BANSHEES), DERYN CORPH (CORPSE BIRDS) AND CŴM ANNWN (HELL HOUNDS).

FOR A SPOOKY RIDE TRY THE STIPERSTONES ROUTE WHICH HAS MORE CREEPY LEGENDS THAN YOU CAN SHAKE A CRUCIFIX AND A BUNCH OF GARLIC AT! (GET SOME LIGHTS AND TRY IT AS A LATE EVENING/NIGHT RIDE IN SUMMER IF YOU'RE REALLY BRAVE!).

THIS IS A FAIRLY EASY SCENIC CRUISE ALONG THE WILD SHORE OF NANT-Y-MOCH RESERVOIR AND AROUND A HANDFUL OF SMALL PICTURESQUE LAKES. THERE ARE NO MAJOR CLIMBS BUT A SHORT ROCKY DESCENT AND A COUPLE OF FORDS ADD A FEW CHALLENGES. IT'S AN IDEAL SUMMER ROUTE - TAKEN GENTLY WITH A PICNIC AND PLENTY OF TIME TO ENJOY THE VIEWS - OR AS A FAST BLAST IN WINTER WHEN IT'S WILD, WET AND WINDSWEPT BUT NOT TOO MUDDY.

IF YOU'RE MORE ADVENTUROUS YOU CAN USE THIS ROUTE AS A BACKBONE FROM WHICH TO BRANCH OFF AND EXPLORE THE NEARBY FORESTS AND MOORS. YOU'LL DISCOVER TRACKS RANGING FROM SMOOTH AND WIDE TO NON-EXISTENT AND VERY BOGGY, PLUS SOME REAL MONSTER FORDS, SO MAKE SURE YOU'VE GOT A GOOD MAP AND WATERPROOF SHOES!

NANT-Y-MOCH RESERVOIR   ROUTE 16

MAP: LANDRANGER 135 OR PATHFINDER 927
DISTANCE: 17½ MILES / 28 KM   **OFFROAD:** 6½ MILES / 10 KM
TIME: 1½ - 2½ HOURS
HIGHEST POINT: 1350 FT / 410 M
TOTAL CLIMBING: 800 FT / 250 M
START: CAR PARK BY NANT-Y-MOCH DAM   755 863

THE ROUTE STARTS BY THE DAM ON NANT-Y-MOCH RESERVOIR.
THIS IS THE LARGEST OF THREE LAKES CREATED ALONG THE AFON
RHEIDOL AS PART OF THE LARGEST HYDRO-ELECTRIC SCHEME IN
ENGLAND AND WALES. (THE DEVIL'S BRIDGE AND VALE OF RHEIDOL ROUTE
TAKES YOU PAST ANOTHER OF THE RESERVOIRS AND THE POWER STATION.)
THE SCHEME PRODUCES ENOUGH ELECTRICITY FOR ABERYSTWYTH AND THE
SURROUNDING AREA.

NEAR THE END OF THE DAM THERE IS A MEMORIAL COMMEMORATING A
NEARBY BATTLE IN WHICH OWAIN GLYNDŴR DEFEATED THE ENGLISH IN 1401.

FROM THE CAR PARK CROSS THE TOP OF THE DAM AND FOLLOW THE ROAD
ALONG THE WESTERN ARM OF THE LAKE. THE ROAD IS NARROW, BUT IT'S
MOSTLY FLAT AND NORMALLY QUIET SO YOU CAN RELAX AND ENJOY THE
VIEWS ACROSS THE RESERVOIR. AFTER ABOUT 3½ MILES (5.5 KM) YOU PASS
THE END OF THE LAKE AND THE VIEW ON THE RIGHT BECOMES BLOCKED
BY TREES. CONTINUE UP THE ROAD FOR A COUPLE OF HUNDRED YARDS
THEN LOOK OUT FOR A CLEAR, WIDE TRACK (ACTUALLY A DERELICT ROAD)
ON YOUR LEFT. (THERE IS A BRIDLEWAY SIGN AT THE END OF THE TRACK
– BUT BEWARE, LAST TIME I WAS HERE IT WAS POINTING THE WRONG WAY!)

Turn onto the track and climb gently for ⅓ mile (0.5 km) to the top of the forest. Continue along a track going straight ahead past a small lake on your left. After another ⅓ mile (0.5 km) bear right where the track forks. Drop down a rough, rocky descent until you meet another track. Follow this track for 2 miles (3 km), through a couple of fords and down to Llyn Syfydrin. Swing right onto the small road by the lake and go through a gate.

Follow the narrow tarmac beyond the lake, ignoring big forest tracks off to either side. When you reach a fork bear right and follow the road between patches of young, mature and clear-felled forest. After ¾ mile (1 km) pass a junction with a small road off to the left and continue up the gentle climb past Llyn Pendam. Stop after a few hundred yards where the road bends round to the right and a superb view opens up all the way down the valley to the sea. (Notice the mining ruins in the bottom of the valley. This area was once dotted with small pits working seams of lead, zinc and silver.)

After gawping at the view turn round and head back down past Llyn Pendam. Turn right at the junction just past the lake. Follow this road for ¾ mile (1 km) until you reach the picturesque Llyn Blaenmelindwr. Turn left at a junction and follow the road around the lake and then up through dark mature forest. When you reach the junction at the top go straight on along the little road back to Llyn Syfydrin. (Bear left after 100 yards where a big forest track forks off to the right.)

Beyond the lake continue back along the track. The rest of the ride retraces the first part of the route from Nant-y-Moch dam. After 2 miles (3 km) turn right up the short rough section of track and continue back towards the forest. Drop down the derelict road through the trees and then turn right at the road junction for the 3½ mile (5.5 km) tarmac cruise along the lake shore back to the dam and car park.

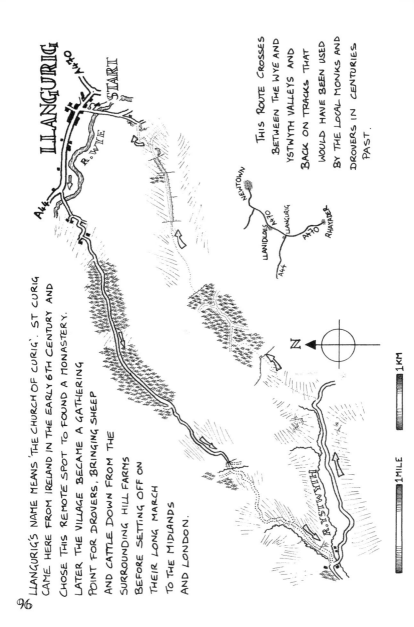

LLANGURIG

START

R. WYE

A44

A470

This route crosses between the Wye and Ystwyth valleys and back on tracks that would have been used by the local monks and drovers in centuries past.

NEWTOWN

LLANIDLOES

A470

LLANGURIG

A44

A44

A470

RHAYADER

N

1 MILE

1 KM

R. YSTWYTH

Llangurig's name means 'the Church of Curig'. St Curig came here from Ireland in the early 6th century and chose this remote spot to found a monastery. Later the village became a gathering point for drovers, bringing sheep and cattle down from the surrounding hill farms before setting off on their long march to the Midlands and London.

LLANGURIG

MAP: LANDRANGER 136. MOST OF THE ROUTE IS ALSO ON LANDRANGER 147 + PATHFINDER 948
DISTANCE: 14½ MILES /22.5 KM   OFFROAD: 6½ MILES / 10 KM
TIME: 1½ – 3 HOURS
HIGHEST POINT: 1755 FT /535 M
TOTAL CLIMBING: 2100 FT / 630 M
START: CAR PARK IN LLANGURIG 908 798

START FROM THE SMALL CAR PARK IN LLANGURIG. TURN RIGHT OUT OF
THE CAR PARK AND THEN LEFT ONTO THE MAIN ROAD THROUGH
THE VILLAGE. RIDE OUT OF THE VILLAGE AND CONTINUE FOR ABOUT
¾ MILE (1KM) UNTIL YOU SEE A SMALL ROAD OFF TO THE LEFT. TURN
LEFT AND FOLLOW THIS ROAD, CROSSING OVER THE RIVER WYE. AFTER
A GENTLE START IT BECOMES A STEADY GRINDING CLIMB FOR 2½ MILES
(4KM), CLIMBING UP TO AND THEN THROUGH A FOREST.

WHAT GOES UP MUST OF COURSE COME DOWN AND THE ROAD
EVENTUALLY ROLLS OVER THE HILLTOP AND PLUNGES INTO THE
VALLEY BEYOND. GO THROUGH THE GATE AT THE END OF THE
ROAD AND SPLASH YOUR WAY THROUGH A ROCKY FORD. THE CLIMB
AFTER THE FORD IS STEEP AND STONY, BUT FORTUNATELY NOT
TOO LONG. AS THE TRACK FLATTENS OUT IT TAKES YOU ACROSS THE
HILL TO THE START OF AN EXCELLENT DESCENT INTO THE YSTWYTH
VALLEY. FAST AND ROCKY WITH A FEW SHARP BENDS, THE TRACK DROPS
560 FT (170 M) IN 1¼ MILES (2 KM) FINALLY POPPING YOU OUT, VIA A
GATE, ONTO THE ROAD.

THIS IS THE MOUNTAIN ROAD FROM RHAYADER TO ABERYSTWYTH.
TURN LEFT AND FOLLOW THE TARMAC, WINDING UP THE VALLEY ABOVE
THE TUMBLING STREAM AND BETWEEN STEEP SLOPES CROWNED
WITH JAGGED CRAGS. AFTER 1½ MILES (2.5KM) THE VALLEY NARROWS
AND THE ROAD CLIMBS BESIDE THE STREAM FOR A FEW HUNDRED
YARDS BEFORE THE VALLEY OPENS OUT AGAIN AND THE ROAD CURVES
ROUND PAST A BOG.

THIS IS THE GORS LWYD BOG – THE REMAINS OF A LAKE THAT FILLED
THIS VALLEY BEFORE THE LAST ICE AGE. IN THE 1970'S THERE WERE
PLANS TO FLOOD IT AGAIN AS THE NORTHERN TIP OF A VAST
EXTENSION OF THE CRAIG GOCH RESERVOIR. FORTUNATELY IT WAS
DECIDED THERE WAS NO DEMAND FOR THE WATER AND THE SCHEME
WAS NEVER BUILT.

AT THE END OF THE BOG TURN LEFT BY A BRIDLEWAY SIGN TO PICK UP
A SMALL TRACK RUNNING JUST ABOVE THE AREA OF LONG MARSH GRASS.
(DON'T FOLLOW THE DIRECTION OF THE SIGN POST-POINTING STRAIGHT
UP THE HILL). THE TRACK CLIMBS GENTLY FOR 1 MILE (1.5 KM) BECOMING
FAINT IN PLACES. (AS LONG AS YOU KEEP HEADING IN THE RIGHT GENERAL
DIRECTION NAVIGATION SHOULDN'T BE TOO MUCH OF A PROBLEM - ALTHOUGH
THERE ARE A COUPLE OF MISLEADING SHEEP TRACKS. MISTY CONDITIONS
COULD MAKE THINGS DIFFICULT HOWEVER - SO UNLESS YOU'RE HAPPY
USING A COMPASS PICK A CLEAR DAY FOR THIS RIDE.) PLENTY OF BUMPS
AND GRASSY TUSSOCKS AND A FEW BOGGY PATCHES PROVIDE A FUN
CHALLENGE (OR A PAIN IN THE BUM - DEPENDING ON YOUR POINT OF VIEW!).

EVENTUALLY YOU SHOULD REACH A PAIR OF GATES WITH A YOUNG FOREST
A LITTLE WAY BEYOND. GO THROUGH THE GATES AND RIDE TO THE TREES
LOOKING FOR A FIRE BREAK DOWN WHICH YOU SHOULD MAKE YOUR WAY.
BUMPY GROUND HIDDEN BENEATH LONG GRASS MAKES THE NEXT ½ MILE
(0.75 KM) SLOW AND TECHNICAL. JUST AS THINGS START TO GET UNRIDEABLE
AND YOU BEGIN TO GET BORED WITH THE CHALLENGE YOU REACH A BIG
FOREST TRACK. TURN RIGHT, DOWN THE SMOOTH TRACK. BEAR LEFT WHERE
ANOTHER TRACK COMES IN FROM THE RIGHT, AND THEN LEFT AGAIN AT THE NEXT
JUNCTION. (WARNING - THE ORDNANCE SURVEY MAP DOESN'T QUITE REFLECT REALITY
WITH THE POSITION OF TRACKS IN THIS FOREST - BUT THEN UNLESS YOU'VE GOT
THE LATEST VERSION OF THE MAP YOU'LL BE THINKING 'WHAT FOREST?' ANYWAY!)
CLIMB UP THE TRACK FOR A HUNDRED YARDS OR SO THEN TURN OFF RIGHT
DOWN ANOTHER FIRE BREAK. SWOOSH THROUGH THE SMOOTH LONG GRASS
TO A GATE THAT TAKES YOU OUT OF THE FOREST.

BEYOND THE GATE CONTINUE ALONG A FAINT MOORLAND TRACK. GRADUALLY
THE TRACK STARTS TO DESCEND WITH SOME GORGEOUS VIEWS AHEAD.
EVENTUALLY THE ROUTE GETS MORE DEFINED AND THE GRADIENT
STEEPENS TO GIVE SOME BRILLIANT FAST FUN DOWN TO A
GATE. BEYOND THE GATE CRUISE ALONG THE SMOOTH CLEAR
TRACK. AFTER ANOTHER GATE YOU SWING LEFT DOWN THE HILLSIDE
FOR A STONY BLAST TOWARDS THE VALLEY BOTTOM. SHORTLY
AFTER ANOTHER GATE BY A LITTLE QUARRY THE TRACK CURVES TO
THE RIGHT. HERE YOU SHOULD GO STRAIGHT ON (PICK YOUR EXIT FROM
THE BIG STONY TRACK CAREFULLY - THE SLOPE IS STEEP). DROP
DOWN THE FIELD ON A FAINT GRASSY TRACK, VIA A ZIG-ZAG, TO AN
OBVIOUS TRACK THAT TAKES YOU TO A GATE. TURN LEFT ON THE
ROAD BEYOND THE GATE AND ROLL DOWN TO A JUNCTION. LEFT
AGAIN AND A COUPLE OF MINUTES RIDING TAKES YOU ACROSS THE
RIVER WYE AND BACK TO LLANGURIG.

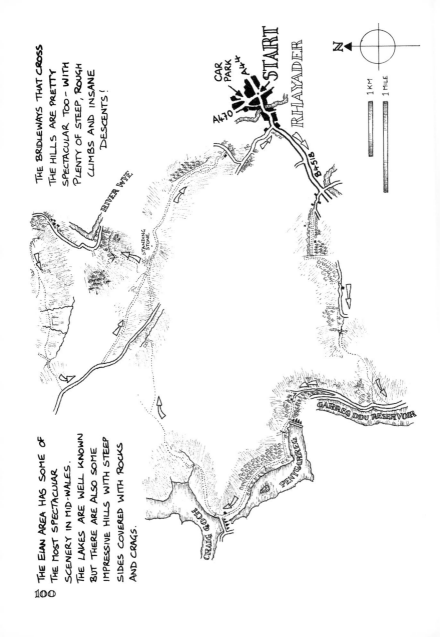

THE BRIDLEWAYS THAT CROSS THE HILLS ARE PRETTY SPECTACULAR TOO - WITH PLENTY OF STEEP, ROUGH CLIMBS AND INSANE DESCENTS!

THE ELAN AREA HAS SOME OF THE MOST SPECTACULAR SCENERY IN MID-WALES. THE LAKES ARE WELL KNOWN BUT THERE ARE ALSO SOME IMPRESSIVE HILLS WITH STEEP SIDES COVERED WITH ROCKS AND CRAGS.

START

RHAYADER

CAR PARK

A44

A470

B4518

N

1 KM

1 MILE

RIVER WYE

STANDING STONE

GARREG DDU RESERVOIR

PENYGARREG

CRAIG GOCH

100

Elan Hills

MAP: LANDRANGER 147 OR PATHFINDERS 948 & 969
DISTANCE: 20 MILES / 32 KM   OFFROAD: 14 MILES / 23 KM
TIME: 3-5 HOURS
HIGHEST POINT: 1600 FT / 490 M
TOTAL CLIMBING: 3300 FT / 1000 M
START: CLOCKTOWER IN CENTRE OF RHAYADER   972 680

FROM THE CENTRE OF RHAYADER HEAD WEST ALONG THE B4518 TOWARDS
THE ELAN VALLEY. AFTER 1¼ MILES (2KM) TURN OFF RIGHT AT A CROSSROADS.
300 YARDS UP THE MINOR ROAD BEAR RIGHT UP A GREEN LANE AND CLIMB
STEADILY UNTIL YOU REACH THE EDGE OF THE OPEN MOORLAND. GO THROUGH
THE GATE AT THE TOP OF THE TRACK AND TURN LEFT ONTO A FAST DESCENT
THAT TAKES YOU DOWN TO THE ROAD. TURN RIGHT AND FOLLOW THE ROAD TO A
GATE. GO THROUGH AND THEN AFTER ⅓ MILE (0.5 KM) LOOK FOR A GATE ON
YOUR RIGHT WITH A BRIDLEWAY SIGN. GO THROUGH AND CLIMB UP THE TRACK
THROUGH THE FIELD, PAST SOME GNARLY OLD TREES. GO THROUGH A GATE
AT THE END OF THE FIELD AND DROP DOWN THROUGH A FORD. FOLLOW THE
MAIN TRACK AS IT ZIGZAGS AND THEN HEADS GENTLY UPWARDS
CLOSE TO THE STREAM. THIS SECTION IS PRETTY ROUGH (I ALWAYS END
UP WALKING!). BEYOND THE ROCKY SECTION THE TRACK BECOMES NARROW
BUT RIDEABLE, UP OVER THE HILLTOP. THE DESCENT DOWN THE FAR SIDE
STARTS AS A FAST WHIZZ ALONG THE NARROW PATH. SUDDENLY YOU
DROP DOWN TO A LITTLE FORD AND MOMENTS LATER YOU'RE STARING
STRAIGHT DOWN THE SCARY-STEEP SLOPE INTO THE ELAN VALLEY, WITH
GARREG-DDU RESERVOIR 400FT (120M) BELOW YOU. THE TRACK IS VERY,
VERY STEEP. MOST OF IT IS RIDEABLE BUT IF YOU VALUE YOUR TEETH AND
UNBROKEN BONES YOU'LL WALK DOWN THE ROUGHEST SECTIONS.

WHEN YOU REACH THE LAKESIDE ROAD (HOPEFULLY STILL IN ONE PIECE!)
TURN RIGHT. AFTER ⅔ MILE (1KM) FORK TO THE RIGHT UP A SMALL ROAD.
BEAR LEFT AT THE NEXT FORK AND DROP DOWN TO JOIN A CLEAR WIDE
TRACK WHICH YOU CAN FOLLOW FOR THE NEXT 1¾ MILES (3KM)
PAST PENYGARREG DAM AND RESERVOIR UNTIL YOU REACH CRAIG GOCH
DAM. DON'T CROSS THE DAM BUT CONTINUE STRAIGHT ON TO A GATE
AND ANOTHER TRACK. AFTER ¾ MILE (1KM) OF GENTLE CLIMBING YOU
SPLASH THROUGH A FORD AND HEAD UP THE STEEP HILLSIDE. FOLLOW
THE FAINT BRIDLEWAY UP OVER THE BLEAK HILLTOP AND DOWN THE
FAR SIDE. A GOOD DESCENT TAKES YOU DOWN PAST SOME SHEEP PENS,
THROUGH A FORD AND THEN UP TO THE ROAD.

TURN RIGHT AND THEN AFTER 200 YARDS BEAR LEFT ONTO ANOTHER BRIDLEWAY. CONTINUE STRAIGHT ON AFTER A COUPLE OF HUNDRED YARDS WHERE THE TRACK MERGES WITH ANOTHER FROM THE RIGHT. FURTHER ON YOU MEET ANOTHER CLEAR TRACK FROM THE LEFT. IF YOU WANT TO MISS OUT THE LOOP DOWN INTO THE WYE VALLEY GO STRAIGHT ON HERE - UP THE SLOPE TOWARDS A STANDING STONE ON THE HILLTOP. OTHERWISE TURN LEFT ACROSS THE MAIN TRACK. CROSS THE FLATTISH AREA TO WHERE THE GROUND DROPS AWAY INTO THE VALLEY. THE ROUTE ISN'T VISIBLE ON THE GROUND HERE - BUT DROP OVER THE STEEP EDGE, NEAR WHERE THE FLAT GROUND RISES UP A SLOPE TO THE LEFT, AND YOU SHOULD SOON PICK UP THE TRACK AS IT CUTS ACROSS THE HILLSIDE AND DROPS INTO THE VALLEY. (A QUICK RECCE ON FOOT FIRST HELPS.) AFTER A STEEP, FAST PLUMMET, BEAR RIGHT AT A FORK AND FOLLOW THE TRACK ALONG BESIDE A FENCE. PARTS OF THIS TRACK GET A BIT OVERGROWN WITH BRACKEN IN LATE SUMMER - BUT IT ALL ADDS TO THE FUN! WHERE THE HILLSIDE SWINGS ROUND TO THE RIGHT, WITH ROCKY CRAGS ON THE SLOPE ABOVE YOU, LOOK FOR A SMALL GATE (WITH A BLUE BRIDLEWAY ARROW ON THE GATEPOST) ON YOUR LEFT. GO THROUGH AND DROP STRAIGHT DOWN THROUGH THE STEEP OAK WOOD TO REACH ANOTHER SMALL GATE OUT ONTO A ROAD.

TURN LEFT AND CRUISE ALONG THE TARMAC FOR 1 MILE (1.5 KM). AFTER PASSING NANNERTH FARM (WATCH OUT FOR THE VERY FREE RANGE CHICKENS!) BEAR LEFT UP A TRACK WITH A BRIDLEWAY SIGN. FOLLOW THE BRIDLEWAY UP PAST SOME GNARLY OLD TREES TO REACH A GATE INTO A FIELD. GO THROUGH AND RIDE STRAIGHT UP THE FIELD TO A STILE. CLIMB OVER AND TURN RIGHT, FOLLOWING THE FENCE TO A GATE. GO THROUGH AND FOLLOW THE CLEAR TRACK, CLIMBING STEADILY FOR ½ MILE (0.75 KM). WHERE THE TRACK FLATTENS OUT LOOK FOR A FAINT FORK WHERE YOU SHOULD BEAR LEFT. A BIT OF FAST, GENTLE DESCENT TAKES YOU DOWN TO A FORD. CONTINUE ALONG THE FAINT TRACK BEYOND, PAST AN OLD STONE SLAB WALL AND THROUGH ANOTHER SMALL FORD. WHEN YOU REACH A CLEAR TRACK TURN LEFT AND FOLLOW IT DOWN THROUGH A FORD AND THEN UP THE SLOPE FOR ⅓ MILE (0.5 KM) TO THE ROAD.

TURN LEFT AND AFTER ⅓ MILE (0.5 KM) OF GENTLE ROAD CLIMBING, BEAR LEFT ONTO A CLEAR TRACK WHERE THE ROAD LEVELS OFF. FOLLOW THIS TRACK ACROSS THE MOORLAND, DROPPING DOWN AFTER 1¼ MILES (2 KM) TO THE PLACE WHERE YOU EARLIER CHOSE TO HEAD DOWN INTO THE WYE VALLEY. CARRY STRAIGHT ON UP THE MAIN TRACK, PAST MAEN SERTH STANDING STONE, TO THE START OF THE FINAL DESCENT. ROUGH, ROCKY AND RUTTED IN PLACES ITS A BRILLIANT 1½ MILE (2.5 KM) BLAST. BEAR LEFT WHEN YOU REACH A FORK, BESIDE A WOOD AND CARRY ON DOWN, THROUGH SOME SHARP BENDS, PAST A HOUSE AND DOWN TO A GATE ONTO THE ROAD. TURN RIGHT ON THE TARMAC AND FOLLOW IT DOWN TO A T-JUNCTION. TURN LEFT, AND THEN LEFT AGAIN AFTER ¾ MILE (1 KM) AND TRUNDLE BACK INTO RHAYADER.

The scary-steep descent to Garreg Ddu Reservoir ▶

THIS ROUTE IS SOMETHING OF A CLASSIC. IT COMBINES
CHALLENGING RIDING ACROSS BLEAK MOORLAND, ALONG
PART OF THE OLD MONK'S ROAD, AND EASY TRACKS
THROUGH DRAMATIC SCENERY AROUND THE
ELAN VALLEY LAKES.

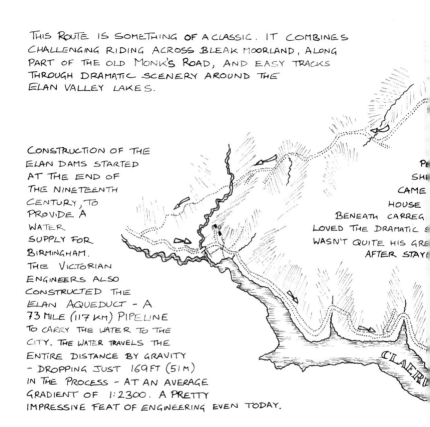

CONSTRUCTION OF THE
ELAN DAMS STARTED
AT THE END OF
THE NINETEENTH
CENTURY, TO
PROVIDE A
WATER
SUPPLY FOR
BIRMINGHAM.
THE VICTORIAN
ENGINEERS ALSO
CONSTRUCTED THE
ELAN AQUEDUCT - A
73 MILE (117 KM) PIPELINE
TO CARRY THE WATER TO THE
CITY. THE WATER TRAVELS THE
ENTIRE DISTANCE BY GRAVITY
- DROPPING JUST 169FT (51M)
IN THE PROCESS - AT AN AVERAGE
GRADIENT OF 1:2300. A PRETTY
IMPRESSIVE FEAT OF ENGINEERING EVEN TODAY.

P·
SH·
CAME
HOUSE
BENEATH CARREG
LOVED THE DRAMATIC S·
WASN'T QUITE HIS GRE·
AFTER STAY·

CLAER·

ELAN'S PEAT BOGS ARE LEGENDARY. EVEN IN MID-SUMMER YOU'LL GET YOUR FEET WET
ON THIS ROUTE. THE BOGGY LANDSCAPE IS A VERY DELICATE NATURAL HABITAT - SO KEEP
TO THE TRACKS TO AVOID SPREADING EROSION

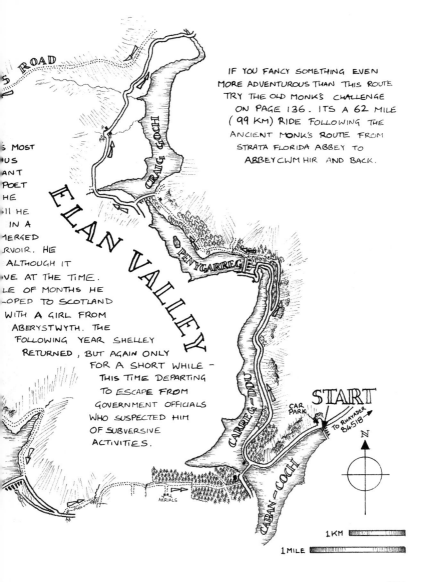

'S ROAD

IF YOU FANCY SOMETHING EVEN MORE ADVENTUROUS THAN THIS ROUTE TRY THE OLD MONK'S CHALLENGE ON PAGE 136. IT'S A 62 MILE (99 KM) RIDE FOLLOWING THE ANCIENT MONK'S ROUTE FROM STRATA FLORIDA ABBEY TO ABBEY CWM HIR AND BACK.

CRAIG GOCH

ELAN VALLEY

PEN Y GARREG

'S MOST
'US
'ANT
POET
HE
'LL HE
IN A
MERGED
'RVOIR. HE
ALTHOUGH IT
'VE AT THE TIME.
'LE OF MONTHS HE
'OPED TO SCOTLAND
WITH A GIRL FROM
ABERYSTWYTH. THE
FOLLOWING YEAR SHELLEY
RETURNED, BUT AGAIN ONLY
FOR A SHORT WHILE –
THIS TIME DEPARTING
TO ESCAPE FROM
GOVERNMENT OFFICIALS
WHO SUSPECTED HIM
OF SUBVERSIVE
ACTIVITIES.

CARREG - DDU

START

CAR PARK

TO RHAYADER B4518

N

CABAN - COCH

AERIALS

1 KM

1 MILE

Elan Lakes

MAP: LANDRANGER 147   OR PATHFINDERS 948 + 969
DISTANCE: 26½ MILES / 42·5 KM   OFFROAD: 18½ MILES / 29 KM
TIME: 4 - 6 HOURS
HIGHEST POINT: 1778 FT / 542 M
TOTAL CLIMBING: 2300 FT / 700 M
START: CABAN - COCH DAM 924 646

START FROM THE CAR PARK IN THE OLD QUARRY BESIDE CABAN-
COCH DAM. TURN RIGHT OUT OF THE CAR PARK AND FOLLOW THE
ROAD ALONG THE LAKESIDE. AFTER 1 MILE (1·5 KM) YOU PASS
CARREG - DDU VIADUCT AND FOEL TOWER, FROM WHERE THE VALLEY'S
WATERS START THEIR JOURNEY DOWN THE PIPELINE TO BIRMINGHAM.

CONTINUE ALONGSIDE CARREG-DDU RESERVOIR UNTIL YOU REACH A
FORK IN THE ROAD. TURN RIGHT AND THEN, AFTER ½ MILE (0·75 KM),
LEFT AT ANOTHER FORK. THE TINY ROAD DROPS DOWN TO THE ROUTE
OF THE OLD DAM CONSTRUCTION RAILWAY WHICH YOU NOW FOLLOW.
THIS TAKES YOU ON A 2 MILE (3 KM) SCENIC CRUISE PAST PENYGARREG
DAM, THROUGH WOODLAND AND A ROCKY CUTTING, AND ALONG THE
LAKESIDE TO CRAIG GOCH DAM.

WHEN YOU REACH CRAIG GOCH CROSS THE DAM AND TURN RIGHT ON
THE ROAD. AFTER 2½ MILES (4 KM) TURN SHARP LEFT ONTO A
FAINT TRACK. (THE ROAD IS UNFENCED HERE, BUT THERE IS A SHORT
STRETCH OF FENCE ACROSS THE END OF THE TRACK TO STOP VEHICLES
FROM GOING UP IT.) AFTER A FEW YARDS TURN LEFT ON A BADLY
RUTTED TRACK. THIS IS PART OF THE OLD MONK'S ROAD AND TAKES
YOU ACROSS 7 MILES (11 KM) OF BLEAK, HIGH MOORLAND.

LOOK OUT FOR SOME OF THE BIRDS THAT LIVE IN THIS WILD
AND INHOSPITABLE LANDSCAPE. THE RED KITES ARE THE MOST
FAMOUS BUT YOU MAY ALSO SEE KESTRELS, BUZZARDS, RAVENS,
MERLINS (NOT THE FANCY TITANIUM VARIETY!) AND GOLDEN PLOVERS. MOST
IMPRESSIVE OF ALL ARE THE PEREGRINES - SMALL BUT INCREDIBLY
POWERFUL FALCONS, CAPABLE OF DIVING AT SPEEDS OF UP TO 200 MPH
(320 KPH) - (IF YOU SEE ONE COMING - DUCK!).

THE MONK'S ROAD IS A FAIRLY WELL USED TRACK AND MOSTLY EASY
TO FOLLOW - ALTHOUGH IT IS BOGGY IN PLACES AND NAVIGATION IS
LIKELY TO BE DIFFICULT IN MISTY CONDITIONS. ABOUT 3 MILES (4·5 KM)
FROM THE TARMAC ROAD KEEP TO THE RIGHT WHERE THE TRACK FORKS.

RIGHT AGAIN ABOUT A MILE (1·5 KM) FURTHER ON, THROUGH A MONSTER PUDDLE AS THE TRACK SWINGS ACROSS THE HEAD OF A VALLEY. THE SQUELCH UNDER YOUR TYRES BECOMES SCRUNCH AS YOU REACH A STONY STRETCH OF TRACK. CONTINUE PAST ROCK OUTCROPS, THEN DOWN A SHORT BUMPY SLOPE BEFORE SWINGING RIGHT FOR ANOTHER BATTLE OF THE BOG AROUND THE HEAD OF A VALLEY. OVER THE FLANK OF THE HILL, IGNORE A TRACK TO THE LEFT AND CONTINUE ALONG THE MAIN TRACK TO A DESCENT TO THE RIVER. KEEP RIGHT TO AVOID A SMOOTH TRACK ALONG THE SIDE OF THE HILL AND DROP DOWN TO THE FORD.

THE FORD IS NOT RIDEABLE. THE BEST WAY ACROSS THE RIVER IS TO PUSH YOUR BIKE INTO THE WATER IN FRONT OF YOU AND USE IT AS A SUPPORT AS YOU LEAP BETWEEN THE ROCKS.

CROSS THE BOG AFTER THE RIVER AND CONTINUE ALONG THE TRACK UNTIL YOU EVENTUALLY REACH ANOTHER, WELL DEFINED, TRACK. TURN LEFT. THIS TRACK HAS SOME TRULY MONSTROUS PUDDLES. (I ONCE SAW SOMEONE CRASH IN ONE - BIKE AND RIDER TOPPLED OVER AND COMPLETELY DISAPPEARED UNDER THE WATER! BEWARE.) AFTER CROSSING THE BRIDGE NEAR CLAERWEN FARM THE TRACK BECOMES A SMOOTH AND GRAVELLY 7 MILE (11 KM) RIDE ALONG THE SIDE OF CLAERWEN RESERVOIR.

CLAERWEN WAS THE LAST ADDITION TO THE ELAN DAMS SCHEME, COMPLETED IN 1952. THE WORKFORCE INCLUDED 100 ITALIAN STONE MASONS. AFTER THE WAR THERE WAS A SHORTAGE OF MASONS AND MOST OF THE SKILLED WORKERS WERE WORKING ON THE REBUILDING OF THE HOUSES OF PARLIAMENT, SO THE DAM BUILDERS HAD TO LOOK MUCH FURTHER AFIELD.

YOU FINALLY REACH TARMAC AGAIN BY THE DAM. DROP DOWN THE FAST 3/4 MILE (1 KM) DESCENT AND TURN LEFT (EFFECTIVELY STRAIGHT ON) AT THE JUNCTION. A FEW YARDS FURTHER ON TURN LEFT ONTO A BRIDLEWAY. FOLLOW THIS TRACK, ABOVE SOME FIELDS, TO A STREAM. CROSS THE STREAM TO A LARGE, SMOOTH TRACK AND TURN LEFT, CLIMBING GENTLY UP THE HILL. FOLLOW THIS TRACK UNTIL IT SWINGS RIGHT TO SOME AERIALS, THEN CONTINUE STRAIGHT ON ACROSS SMOOTH GRASS BY THE EDGE OF A FOREST. WHEN YOU REACH A CORNER GO THROUGH THE GATE INTO THE WOODLAND. THIS TRACK BECOMES A BRILLIANT WILD AND SLIPPERY MUDSLIDE, DROPPING STRAIGHT DOWN THROUGH THE FOREST TO THE ROAD BESIDE CABAN-COCH RESERVOIR. TURN LEFT, CROSS THE VIADUCT AND THEN TURN RIGHT BACK TO THE START.

TO FIND OUT MORE ABOUT THE RESERVOIRS, HISTORY AND WILDLIFE OF ELAN DROP IN AT THE EXCELLENT VISITOR CENTRE AT THE BOTTOM OF CABAN-COCH DAM. THERE'S ALSO A CAFE THERE IF YOU JUST WANT TO REFUEL YOUR BODY.

MOORLAND BIRDS

RIDING IN WILD COUNTRYSIDE YOU'LL GET SOME BRILLIANT CHANCES TO SEE WILDLIFE. THESE ARE A FEW OF THE MORE INTERESTING BIRDS TO LOOK OUT FOR.

BUZZARD.

AN EAGLE-LIKE BIRD OF PREY. OFTEN SEEN IN HILL COUNTRY SOARING MAJESTICALLY ON THEIR BROAD WINGS. THEY ARE SOMETIMES DRAMATICALLY 'MOBBED' BY GROUPS OF SMALLER BIRDS WHICH TRY TO CHASE THE BUZZARD AWAY FROM THEIR NESTS.

RED KITE.

ONE OF BRITAIN'S RAREST BIRDS. LIKE THE BUZZARD BUT WITH A DISTINCTIVE FORKED TAIL. YOU MAY BE LUCKY ENOUGH TO SEE ONE ON SOME OF THE MORE REMOTE WELSH RIDES.

KESTREL.

THESE SMALL BIRDS OF PREY CAN BE FOUND THROUGHOUT THE COUNTRYSIDE. THEY ARE OFTEN SEEN HOVERING AS THEY SEARCH THE GROUND FOR SMALL ANIMALS WHICH THEY DIVE ONTO TO CATCH.

RAVEN.

AN OVERSIZED MEMBER OF THE CROW FAMILY. WATCH THEM IN THE SPRING WHEN THEY GIVE AMAZING AEROBATIC DISPLAYS – LOOPING AND ROLLING ACROSS THE SKY – TO ATTRACT A PARTNER. ALTHOUGH CAPABLE OF KILLING RATS AND RABBITS THEY USUALLY PREFER TO SCAVENGE FROM DEAD ANIMALS – (DON'T SIT STILL FOR TOO LONG!).

RED GROUSE.

THE FIRST YOU'LL SEE OF A GROUSE IS WHEN IT EXPLODES OUT OF THE HEATHER IN FRONT OF YOU, AND FLAPS OFF GIVING IT'S LOUD CACKLING CRY. LOOK OUT ALSO FOR BLACK GROUSE (THE FEMALE IS CONFUSINGLY BROWN- SIMILAR TO THE RED GROUSE). THE RED GROUSE HAS BECOME FAIRLY RARE. (SOME SHOOTERS CLAIM WALKERS AND MOUNTAIN BIKERS ARE TO BLAME – NOTHING TO DO WITH THEM BLASTING THE POOR THINGS OUT OF THE SKY OF COURSE!).

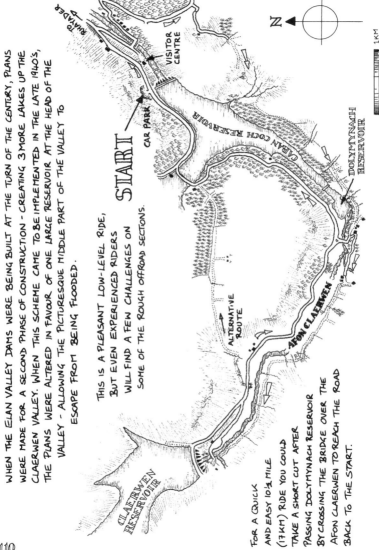

WHEN THE ELAN VALLEY DAMS WERE BEING BUILT AT THE TURN OF THE CENTURY, PLANS WERE MADE FOR A SECOND PHASE OF CONSTRUCTION - CREATING 3 MORE LAKES UP THE CLAERWEN VALLEY. WHEN THIS SCHEME CAME TO BE IMPLEMENTED IN THE LATE 1940's, THE PLANS WERE ALTERED IN FAVOUR OF ONE LARGE RESERVOIR AT THE HEAD OF THE VALLEY - ALLOWING THE PICTURESQUE MIDDLE PART OF THE VALLEY TO ESCAPE FROM BEING FLOODED.

THIS IS A PLEASANT LOW-LEVEL RIDE, BUT EVEN EXPERIENCED RIDERS WILL FIND A FEW CHALLENGES ON SOME OF THE ROUGH OFFROAD SECTIONS.

FOR A QUICK AND EASY 10½ MILE (17 KM) RIDE YOU COULD TAKE A SHORT CUT AFTER PASSING DOLYMYNACH RESERVOIR BY CROSSING THE BRIDGE OVER THE AFON CLAERWEN TO REACH THE ROAD BACK TO THE START.

TO RHAYADER

VISITOR CENTRE

CAR PARK

START

CABAN COCH RESERVOIR

DOLYMYNACH RESERVOIR

ALTERNATIVE ROUTE

AFON CLAERWEN

CLAERWEN RESERVOIR

N

1 KM

1 MILE

110

CLAERWEN VALLEY

MAP: LANDRANGER 147 OR PATHFINDER 969
DISTANCE: 16 MILES/25.5 KM   OFFROAD: 5½ MILES/8.5 KM - OR 7¾ MILES/12.5 KM
TIME: 1½ - 2½ HOURS
HIGHEST POINT: 1350FT/412 M
TOTAL CLIMBING: 1400FT/420M - OR 1800FT/550M
START: CABAN-COCH DAM   924 646

START FROM THE CAR PARK IN THE OLD QUARRY BESIDE CABAN-COCH DAM.
TURN LEFT ONTO THE ROAD AND FOLLOW IT DOWN THE VALLEY AWAY FROM
THE RESERVOIR. AFTER ¾ MILE (1KM) TURN SHARP RIGHT, DOWN THE ROAD
SIGNED TOWARDS THE ELAN VALLEY VISITOR CENTRE. CROSS THE BRIDGE AND
TRUNDLE BACK DOWN THE VALLEY, BESIDE THE TREE-LINED BANKS OF THE AFON
ELAN AND PAST THE HOUSES OF ELAN VILLAGE (BUILT TO REPLACE HOMES LOST
IN THE FLOODING OF THE VALLEY). AT A JUNCTION - SIGNED TO LLANWRTHWL IN
BOTH DIRECTIONS! - TURN RIGHT AND HEAD BACK UP THE VALLEY. FOLLOW
THIS ROAD FOR A MILE (1.5KM), THROUGH PICTURESQUE WOODLAND, THEN
TURN RIGHT DOWN AN EVEN SMALLER SIDE ROAD (WATCH OUT FOR THE GATE
JUST ROUND THE FIRST BEND). AFTER A SHORT LEVEL SECTION THE ROAD
CLIMBS STEEPLY UP THE HILLSIDE. SLOG YOUR WAY UPWARDS UNTIL YOU REACH
THE END OF THE TARMAC AND A GATE.

GO THROUGH THE GATE, OUT ONTO THE OPEN MOORLAND, AND CONTINUE
STRAIGHT ON, UP A ROUGH LOOKING TRACK. THE TRACK SOON SMOOTHS OUT
OVER THE BROW OF THE HILL. AS YOU START TO DESCEND TOWARDS A
RUINED FARMHOUSE BY A CLUMP OF TREES, BEAR LEFT ONTO A GRASSY
TRACK. SCOOT DOWN PAST THE LEFT HAND SIDE OF THE RUIN AND
FOLLOW THE TRACK DOWN THROUGH 3 SPLASHY FORDS. SWING RIGHT
TOWARDS A FORESTRY PLANTATION AND THEN FOLLOW THE EDGE OF THE
FOREST, UP A GENTLE RISE AND THEN DOWN A GOOD, FAST DESCENT. LOOK
OUT ON THE RIGHT FOR OCCASIONAL GLIMPSES THROUGH THE TREES OF
CABAN-COCH RESERVOIR, IN THE VALLEY BELOW.

AFTER CROSSING A FORD GO THROUGH A GATE. CONTINUE STRAIGHT ON ACROSS
A FIELD, HEADING DIAGONALLY DOWNWARDS, FOLLOWING A BARELY VISIBLE HINT
OF A PATH. AT THE FAR END OF THE FIELD YOU PICK UP A CLEAR TRACK, THROUGH
A GATE AND ANOTHER FORD. FOLLOW THIS TRACK DOWN THROUGH A COUPLE
OF FIELDS, THROUGH YET ANOTHER FORD AND ALONG PAST THE SHORE OF
DOLYMYNACH RESERVOIR. DOLYMYNACH WAS PLANNED FOR CONSTRUCTION
DURING THE SECOND PHASE OF THE ELAN SCHEME. THE DAM WAS TO BE
LOCATED ACROSS THE END OF CABAN-COCH RESERVOIR, SO ITS FOUNDATIONS
HAD TO BE BUILT BEFORE CABAN-COCH FILLED AND FLOODED THE AREA.

When the Claerwen Valley plans came to be implemented in the late 1940's, the original scheme was abandoned and a single large dam was built further up the valley. The small lake formed by the foundations of Dolymynach Dam has a peaceful and natural appearance and is a haven for wildlife.

Continue along the track past some farm buildings, then when you reach tarmac turn sharp left. The little road doubles back towards a barn then turns sharp right and wiggles up the valley for ½ mile (0.75km) to another farm. Go through the farmyard, past some barns on your right and then swing round to the right and through a gate. The next 2½ miles (4km) are easy to follow but challenging to ride with rocky sections, boggy bits and fords. Keep following the obvious track up the valley. The scenery is picturesque with steep valley sides and glimpses of the rocky river down to your right - but you'll soon find you need to apply all your concentration to the rocky track. Gradually the valley takes on a more bleak and rugged appearance and as the huge Claerwen Dam becomes visible up ahead the track begins to get boggy with plenty of puddles and fords (beware - after wet weather some of these puddles get seriously deep!) Eventually you reach a wide (but rideable) ford across a tributary of the Afon Claerwen. Beyond the ford, cross a field to a gate and then turn right and cross the bridge. Follow the road past a car park and along to a junction.

Turn left here to ride up to the top of the dam. Claerwen Dam was built in the late 1940's and opened in 1952. In the post-war period there was a shortage of skilled labour in Britain. Many people were still serving in the armed forces and the construction industry was busy repairing wartime bomb damage - so stonemasons and other workers were recruited from as far away as Italy and Poland to work at Claerwen.

After admiring the dam and the contrasting views up and down the valley, return down the road to the junction. Turn left (effectively straight on). After 100 yards you have a choice - either turn left onto a bridleway which climbs up over the hill and slithers down through a forest to Carreg-Ddu Viaduct. (For route details turn to page 107 and follow the last two paragraphs of the Elan Lakes route). - or continue along the smooth flat road down the valley. After crossing Carreg-Ddu viaduct turn right and follow the road along the side of Caban-Coch reservoir back to the start.

Approaching Claerwen Dam - in mid-summer! ▶

Their are two main types of trees - broadleaves such as oak, ash, beech etc and conifers such as firs, pines and spruces.

JAPANESE LARCH

HAZEL

Most native trees in Britain are broadleaved. In some places these still grow in ancient woodlands that have survived since the days when most of Britain was covered with trees. Early settlers began to fell the trees thousands of years ago for fuel and timber and to clear land for farms and villages. In recent centuries the few remaining woods had to be managed in a more sustainable way, with replanting and limited felling in order to maintain supplies. Nowadays most ancient woodlands have been allowed to return to nature as the demands for timber are met by new conifer plantations.

ASH

NORWAY SPRUCE

BEECH

Forestry is a long term exercise - planting trees now to meet demand decades into the future. Trees are grown from seeds in nurseries and planted in the forest at about two years old. After 20 years the young trees are thinned, removing some to allow the better ones more space to grow. Thinning continues every 5 years until the mature crop is finally felled, and the forest replanted, when it reaches 50-60 years old. Felled timber is taken away for a wide range of uses, from building materials to paper making (not to mention Christmas trees!). The average person in Britain uses the equivalent of one large tree each year. So in your lifetime you'll use a small forest - of trees that take a life time to grow!

DOUGLAS FIR

OAK

HORSE CHESTNUT (CONKER TREE)

SCOTS PINE

WARNING! - Commercial forests are working environments. Keep to the rights of way and avoid areas that are being worked in.

THINGS TO SEE ~ WOODLAND CREATURES

FORESTS OFFER A SAFE HIDING PLACE AND PLENTIFUL SUPPLY OF FOOD FOR A WIDE RANGE OF WILDLIFE - FROM TINY INSECTS TO HERDS OF DEER. RIDE QUIETLY AND KEEP YOUR EYES OPEN.

GREY SQUIRREL.

SQUIRRELS ARE THE MOST OBVIOUS WOODLAND ANIMALS YOU'RE LIKELY TO SEE. ORIGINALLY FROM NORTH AMERICA, THE GREY IS NOW FAR MORE COMMON THAN THE NATIVE RED SQUIRREL. ON THE GROUND THEY LOOK LIKE CARTOONS - BUT WATCH OUT FOR THEIR ACROBATIC SKILLS WHEN THEY GET UP INTO THE TREES.

RABBIT.
NOT SPECIFICALLY WOODLAND CREATURES, RABBITS CAN BE FOUND JUST ABOUT EVERYWHERE IN THE COUNTRYSIDE. LIKE THE GREY SQUIRREL THEY ARE NOT NATIVE TO BRITAIN BUT WERE PROBABLY INTRODUCED FROM EUROPE IN ROMAN TIMES. ORIGINALLY THEY WERE KEPT FOR FOOD IN LARGE ARTIFICIAL WARRENS. ONLY IN THE LAST FEW CENTURIES HAVE THEY SPREAD WIDELY IN THE WILD.

FALLOW DEER.
PROBABLY THE BIGGEST WILD CREATURES YOU'RE LIKELY TO SEE. DESPITE THEIR SIZE THEY ARE VERY SHY ANIMALS, BUT CAN OCCASIONALLY BE SEEN GRAZING IN CLEARINGS OR RUNNING ACROSS THE TRACK.

GREAT SPOTTED WOODPECKER.
MORE LIKELY TO BE HEARD THAN SEEN. ONCE YOU'VE REALISED THE KNOCKING NOISE ISN'T COMING FROM YOUR BIKE, PEER UP INTO THE TREETOPS AND YOU MAY CATCH A GLIMPSE OF IT. LOOK OUT ALSO FOR THE GREEN WOODPECKER.

GOLDCREST.
BRITAIN'S SMALLEST BIRD - JUST 3½ INCHES (9CM) FROM THE TIP OF ITS BEAK TO THE END OF ITS TAIL. IT IS USUALLY FOUND IN CONIFER FORESTS, BEING ONE OF THE FEW SPECIES THAT PREFER THE DENSE COMMERCIAL PLANTATIONS TO NATURAL BROADLEAF WOODLANDS.

THIS SHORT RIDE SHOULD BE WITHIN THE CAPABILITIES OF MOST RIDERS
- MAKING IT AN IDEAL ROUTE FOR NOVICES. PICK A SUNNY DAY, PACK A
PICNIC AND MAKE AN AFTERNOON OF IT. THERE'S PLENTY OF FUN
FOR MORE EXPERIENCED RIDERS AS WELL THOUGH - HIGHLY RECOMMENDED
FOR AN EVENING RIDE IN THE SUMMER.

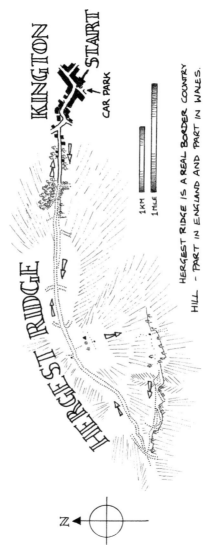

HERGEST RIDGE IS A REAL BORDER COUNTRY
HILL - PART IN ENGLAND AND PART IN WALES.

BUT HERE THE BORDER IS MORE THAN JUST A LINE ON A MAP. LOOKING
EAST FROM THE HILLTOP YOU GAZE ACROSS HEREFORDSHIRE WITH ITS GENTLY
ROLLING HILLS AND PRETTY VILLAGES. TURN WEST AND THE VIEW IS DOMINATED
BY THE HUGE HILLS AND BLEAK MOORLAND OF THE CONTRASTING WELSH
LANDSCAPE.

HERGEST RIDGE

MAP: LANDRANGER 148   OR PATHFINDER 993
DISTANCE: 9½ MILES / 15 KM   OFFROAD: 7 MILES / 11 KM
TIME: 1-2 HOURS
HIGHEST POINT: 1395 FT / 425 M
TOTAL CLIMBING: 1400 FT / 430 M
START: KINGTON - CARPARK IN MILL ST (BY INFORMATION CENTRE) 296 565

FROM THE CLOCKTOWER AT THE END OF MILL STREET, TURN
LEFT AND RIDE UP THE MAIN STREET. PAST THE CHURCH TURN
UP THE SECOND ROAD ON THE LEFT, SIGNED TO RIDGEBOURNE
AND HERGEST CROFT GARDENS. CLIMB.

AFTER 2/3 MILE (1 KM) THE ROAD BECOMES A TRACK LEADING TO
A GATE. THROUGH THE GATE YOU EMERGE ONTO OPEN MOORLAND.
CONTINUE CLIMBING UP THE MAIN TRACK (IGNORE THE TRACK THAT BEARS
RIGHT FROM THE GATE).

FOR THE NEXT 1½ MILES (2.5 KM) YOU SIMPLY FOLLOW THIS TRACK
UP THE SLOPE AND THEN ALONG THE HILLTOP. (THE TRACK SPLITS INTO
A COUPLE OF PARALLEL PATHS IN SOME PLACES - ALL GOING THE SAME
WAY - BUT AVOID TRACKS THAT HEAD SHARPLY OFF AROUND OR DOWN
THE HILL.) THE CLIMB IS LONG BUT NOT TOO STEEP AND YOUR
EFFORTS ARE REWARDED WITH SUPERB VIEWS. AS THE GROUND
FLATTENS OFF ON THE SUMMIT PLATEAU YOU PASS A GROUP OF SMALL
MONKEY PUZZLE TREES (THE PUZZLE FOR ALL YOU MONKEYS OUT
THERE BEING - WHAT ARE THEY DOING UP HERE?). CONTINUE UNTIL
YOU REACH A TALL SIGNPOST WHERE THE TRACK BEGINS TO SLOPE
DOWN TOWARDS THE FAR END OF THE HILL.

THE SIGN INDICATES A BRIDLEWAY OFF TO YOUR LEFT- WHICH YOU
WANT TO TAKE - BUT THERES NOT MUCH SIGN OF IT ON THE GROUND. GO BACK
ABOUT 50 YARDS AND YOU SHOULD FIND A FAINT TRACK
THROUGH THE ANKLE DEEP GORSE. GO THROUGH AND RIDE ACROSS
THE FLAT HILLTOP. ON YOUR RIGHT YOU'LL SEE A PILE OF STONES.
TO YOUR LEFT IS ANOTHER AND BEYOND THAT THERE IS A THIRD BY A
TRIG POINT. AIM FOR THE MIDDLE PILE OF ROCKS AND THEN KEEP
GOING, LOOKING FOR A SMALL WOODEN SIGNPOST.

FROM THE POST THE ROUTE GOES STRAIGHT DOWN THE HILL. IN SOME
PLACES YOU MAY FIND TRACES OF AN OLD SUNKEN TRACK - BUT FOR
MOST OF THE WAY IT SEEMS TO HAVE SUNK WITHOUT TRACE! - SO AIM

ROUGHLY FOR THE MIDDLE OF A LONG WOOD YOU CAN SEE ON A FACING SLOPE IN THE BOTTOM OF THE VALLEY AND CONCENTRATE ON PICKING THE LEAST PRICKLY ROUTE THROUGH THE GORSE MAZE. AFTER A BIT YOU SHOULD SEE A FENCE AND - IF YOU'VE BEEN HEADING THE RIGHT WAY - A TALL SIGN POST. AT THE SIGN POST TURN RIGHT AND RIDE ALONG THE HILLSIDE - STAYING AT ROUGHLY THE SAME HEIGHT AND PICKING YOUR WAY THROUGH A FEW MORE BITS OF GORSE.

(I KNOW THIS ALL SOUNDS LIKE A NAVIGATIONAL NIGHTMARE BUT IT'S ACTUALLY PRETTY EASY. FROM THE MAIN TRACK YOU CUT ACROSS THE HILLTOP ROUGHLY AT A RIGHT ANGLE AND THEN JUST HEAD DOWN. THE GORSE MAZE CAN BE BRILLIANT FUN - ESPECIALLY IF YOU'RE WITH A BUNCH OF COMPETITIVE FRIENDS! GRAVITY WILL GUIDE YOU DOWN THE SLOPE AND IT DOESN'T REALLY MATTER WHERE YOU MEET THE FENCE - AS LONG AS YOU TURN RIGHT YOU CAN'T GO WRONG.)

CONTINUE ALONG THE HILLSIDE UNTIL YOU REACH THE TOP CORNER OF A FENCE COMING UP THE SLOPE. FOLLOW THE FENCE ABOVE THE TOP OF A FIELD FOR A SHORT DISTANCE UNTIL YOU FIND A CLEARLY DEFINED TRACK THAT SWOOPS DOWN TO THE RIGHT INTO A SMALL VALLEY. AS YOU SHOOT ACROSS THE VALLEY BOTTOM YOU CROSS THE BORDER FROM ENGLAND INTO WALES, THEN TAKE A SHORT RUTTED CLIMB UP THE SLOPE BEYOND. OUT OF THE LITTLE VALLEY THE TRACK SPLITS 3 WAYS. TAKE THE LEFT-HAND PATH AND FOLLOW IT ALONG THE HILLSIDE UNTIL YOU EVENTUALLY EMERGE ONTO THE NARROW BROW OF THE WESTERN END OF THE HILL. TURN RIGHT AND THEN ALMOST IMMEDIATELY BEAR RIGHT AT A FORK TO FOLLOW THE OFFA'S DYKE PATH UP THE HILL.

1 MILE (1.5 KM) OF NOT TOO STRENUOUS CLIMBING BRINGS YOU BACK UP ONTO THE FLAT HILLTOP. CONTINUE STRAIGHT ON PAST THE SIGN POST WHERE YOU EARLIER TURNED OFF THROUGH THE GORSE AND ALONG PAST THE LITTLE MONKEY PUZZLES. THEN IT'S YOUR LAST CHANCE TO ADMIRE THE VIEW BEFORE YOU FOCUS ON THE FINAL BRILLIANT DESCENT - DROPPING 890 FT (270 M) IN 2½ MILES (4 KM) BACK TO THE CAR PARK (AND PUBS!) IN KINGTON.

(WATCH OUT FOR PONIES, SHEEP, PEOPLE AND DOGS (AND DOG CRAP!) ON THE FAST GRASSY TRACKS - AND CARS COMING OUT OF HERGEST CROFT GARDENS ON THE ROAD.)

AT FIRST GLANCE RADNOR FOREST SEEMS LIKE AN ODD NAME FOR A MOUNTAIN. IN MEDIEVAL TIMES THE WORD 'FOREST' MEANT A ROYAL HUNTING AREA. MANY OF THESE FORESTS WERE COVERED WITH TREES - LEADING TO THE MODERN MEANING OF THE WORD - BUT AT RADNOR THE FOREST WAS A BLEAK, TREELESS MOUNTAIN AND MOORLAND. JUST TO CONFUSE THINGS FOREST ENTERPRISE NOW HAVE A LARGE PLANTATION COVERING PART OF THE MOUNTAIN - SO IT'S A FOREST IN THE TRADITIONAL AND MODERN SENSE.

RADNOR FOREST

RADNOR FOREST IS AN EXCELLENT PLACE FOR MOUNTAIN BIKING. THIS ROUTE INCLUDES BIG CLIMBS, BRILLIANT DESCENTS, WILD COUNTRYSIDE, SUPERB VIEWS AND JUST 1/4 MILE (0.5 KM) OF ROAD.

N

1 KM
1 MILE

NEW RADNOR
1 1/2 MILES
2.5 KM

A44

START

Radnor Forest

MAP: LANDRANGER 148 . PATHFINDERS 970 (AND A BIT ON 992)
DISTANCE: 16 MILES / 25.5KM   OFFROAD: 15¾ MILES / 25KM
TIME: 2½ – 4 HOURS
HIGHEST POINT: 2150FT / 650M
TOTAL CLIMBING: 2600FT / 800M
START: CAR PARK OFF A44 NEAR NEW RADNOR   194 593

PARK IN THE SMALL CAR PARK JUST OFF THE A44 1½ MILES (2.5KM) SOUTH-WEST
OF NEW RADNOR . FROM THE CAR PARK FOLLOW THE CLEAR, WIDE TRACK HEADING
AWAY FROM THE ROAD . AFTER ½ MILE (0.75KM) BEAR LEFT AT A FORK AND
CLIMB UP THROUGH SOME WOODLAND. CONTINUE ALONG THE BYWAY (WAYMARKED
WITH LITTLE RED ARROWS) BEYOND THE TREES AND UP THROUGH FIELDS FOR ANOTHER
1¼ MILES (2KM). WHEN YOU REACH A PAIR OF GATES SIDE BY SIDE, GO THROUGH THE GATE ON
THE LEFT AND CONTINUE STRAIGHT ON, ACROSS ROUGH MOORLAND, FOLLOWING THE FENCE
ON YOUR RIGHT. (BEWARE - THERE ARE SOME DEEP PUDDLES ALONG THIS BIT OF
TRACK). AFTER CROSSING A SMALL FORD ABOVE A NARROW, ROCKY GORGE, FOLLOW
THE TRACK THROUGH A GATE, THEN GO THROUGH THE NEXT GATE ON YOUR RIGHT AND
CLIMB THE STEEP HILL, KEEPING THE FENCE ON YOUR LEFT.

EVENTUALLY, WITH A BRILLIANT PANORAMA OF DISTANT HILLS ON YOUR LEFT, YOU REACH
THE TOP OF THE CLIMB. CONTINUE ALONG THE TRACK FOR ANOTHER 1½ MILES (2.5KM)
- MOSTLY SMOOTH, FAST DOWNHILL - UNTIL YOU MEET A GATE. FOLLOW THE TRACK DOWN
PAST FIELDS AND A BARN UNTIL YOU EMERGE ONTO A (VERY) MINOR ROAD.

ROLL DOWN THE TARMAC FOR 500 YARDS AND GO STRAIGHT ON - ONTO A CLEAR
TRACK WHERE THE ROAD BENDS TO THE RIGHT. SPLASH DOWN THROUGH THE
PUDDLES AND THEN SHORTLY AFTER A LEFT BEND TURN RIGHT, ONTO A FLAT
GRASSY TRACK. TRUNDLE ALONG UNTIL YOU MEET THE LITTLE ROAD AGAIN.
CROSS THE ROAD ONTO A FARM TRACK. AFTER A COUPLE OF HUNDRED YARDS
IGNORE A TRACK GOING STEEPLY DOWN TO YOUR LEFT AND CONTINUE UP PAST A BARN,
THROUGH A COUPLE OF GATES AND DOWN THE SIDE OF A FIELD TO A TRACK JUNCTION.
TURN RIGHT AND THEN BEAR LEFT THROUGH A GATE ONTO A TRACK WHICH
DROPS DOWN BETWEEN HIGH HEDGES TO A COUPLE OF GATES. GO THROUGH, PAST
A FISH POND AND AN ORNAMENTAL GATEWAY, AND FOLLOW THE TRACK STRAIGHT
ON, BESIDE A WALL AND THEN UP THE EDGE OF A FIELD. AT THE TOP OF
THE FIELD, WITH A PATCH OF WOODLAND ON YOUR RIGHT, YOU NEED
TO BEAR LEFT OFF THE MAIN TRACK, BY A BARN. FOLLOW THE
HEDGE TO A SMALL GATE, AND THEN SHORTLY AFTER, SWING RIGHT BACK
ONTO THE MAIN GRASSY TRACK. DROP DOWN TO ANOTHER GATE AND FOLLOW
THE TRACK BEYOND TO A JUNCTION.

TURN RIGHT AT THE JUNCTION. AFTER 300 YARDS TAKE THE RIGHT-HAND GATE WHERE THE TRACK FORKS AND CONTINUE ALONG THE TRACK, CLIMBING UP THE HILL, WITH FORESTRY LAND ON YOUR LEFT. SHORTLY AFTER PASSING THROUGH A GATEWAY, BEAR LEFT OFF THE TRACK TO A SMALL GATE AND GO THROUGH INTO FORESTRY LAND. CONTINUE UP THE HILL, FOLLOWING THE FENCE ON YOUR RIGHT. THE TRACK HERE IS LITTLE USED, AND WITH BUMPY GROUND HIDDEN BENEATH LONG GRASS IT CAN BE QUITE TRICKY. IT'S MOSTLY RIDEABLE THOUGH - SO KEEP STRUGGLING ON UPWARDS. EVENTUALLY WHEN RIDING BECOMES COMPLETELY IMPOSSIBLE, LOOK OUT FOR A SMALL SIGNPOST ABOVE YOU ON THE LEFT AND SCRAMBLE UP ONTO A SMOOTH, WIDE FOREST TRACK.

TURN RIGHT AND FOLLOW THE LARGE TRACK FOR ABOUT 200 YARDS, THEN SWING LEFT ONTO A SMALL TRACK THAT DISAPPEARS UP A STEEP, DARK GAP BETWEEN THE TREES. THIS IS A LONG, STEEP CLIMB WITH SOME ROUGH SECTIONS HIGHER UP. A COMPLETE ASCENT WITHOUT GETTING OFF TO REST OR WALK IS A REAL CHALLENGE REQUIRING IMPRESSIVE LEGS, LUNGS AND RIDING SKILLS. IGNORE A TRACK TO THE LEFT HALFWAY UP AND KEEP CLIMBING. A CLEAR FELLED AREA ON YOUR LEFT GIVES GOOD VIEWS ACROSS THE WOODLAND (AND A GOOD EXCUSE TO STOP FOR A REST!). FURTHER ON YOU PASS A CLEAR FELLED AREA ON YOUR RIGHT. AT THE END OF THIS THE TRACK BENDS TO THE LEFT AND LEVELS OFF - BUT YOU NEED TO CONTINUE STRAIGHT ON, UP A ROUGH FIRE BREAK BETWEEN THE TREES. AT THE END OF THE FIRE BREAK, TURN RIGHT ONTO A SMALL TRACK AND FOLLOW IT, TWISTING THROUGH THE TREES AND SPLASHING THROUGH DEEP PUDDLES UNTIL IT LEADS YOU TO A GATE OUT ONTO THE OPEN HILLTOP.

BEYOND THE GATE GO STRAIGHT ON ALONG A FAINT TRACK. THE TRACK TAKES YOU SHORTLY TO A FENCE WHICH YOU FOLLOW ON YOUR RIGHT ACROSS THE BLEAK HILLTOP. IGNORE A TRACK FORKING OFF TO THE LEFT AND CONTINUE ALONGSIDE THE FENCE UNTIL YOU REACH A GATE. GO THROUGH AND CARRY ON, WITH THE FENCE ON YOUR LEFT NOW. THE FENCE AND TRACK SWING TO THE LEFT, THEN AS THEY CURVE BACK TO THE RIGHT LOOK FOR A SLIGHTLY SUNKEN TRACK ON YOUR RIGHT. THIS IS THE START OF A BRILLIANT, BUMPY 3/4 MILE (1KM) DESCENT. (RIDE IT FAST AND YOU'LL END UP WITH EITHER A BIG GRIN OR SOME BIG BRUISES!)

AT THE TRACK JUNCTION AT THE BOTTOM YOU REJOIN THE FIRST PART OF THE ROUTE FOR THE RETURN BACK TO THE START. A SHORT CLIMB TAKES YOU BACK OVER A BROW OF THE HILL AND THEN IT'S 3½ MILES (5.5 KM) MOSTLY DOWNHILL BACK TO THE CAR PARK. (WATCH OUT FOR THE GULLIES LURKING IN THE SHADOWS ON THE FINAL SECTION DOWN THROUGH THE WOOD - DEADLY IF YOU HIT THEM AT WARP SPEED!)

THIS IS CLASSIC MID-WALES. WILD HILL COUNTRY,
FARMLAND AND A SCATTERING OF TINY, PEACEFUL
VILLAGES. THERE ARE SOME GOOD TRACKS TOO
— OFFERING ENJOYABLE RIDING AND PLENTY
OF VIEWS AS THEY CROSS THE HIGH GROUND

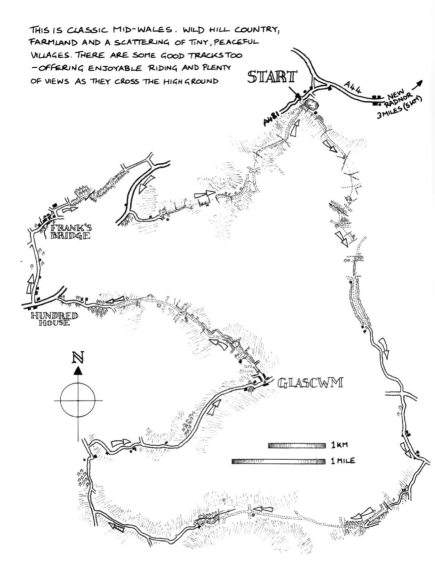

START

A44

NEW
RADNOR
3 MILES (5 KM)

A481

FRANK'S
BRIDGE

HUNDRED
HOUSE

N

GLASCWM

1 KM

1 MILE

GLASCWM

MAP: LANDRANGER 148 OR PATHFINDER 992
DISTANCE: 25½ MILES / 41 KM   OFFROAD: 12½ MILES / 20 KM
TIME: 3-5 HOURS
HIGHEST POINT: 1550 FT / 480 M
TOTAL CLIMBING: 3300 FT / 1000 M
START: SMALL CAR PARK BESIDE A481   166 582

SET OFF ALONG THE OBVIOUS TRACK PAST THE LAKE. CONTINUE PAST A BARN
AND UP THE HILLSIDE. HALFWAY UP GO THROUGH A GATE AND KEEP CLIMBING
TO REACH ANOTHER GATE UP ON THE HILLTOP. GO THROUGH AND AFTER A FEW
YARDS GO THROUGH ANOTHER GATE IN THE FENCE ON YOUR LEFT. CROSS THIS FIELD
HEADING DIAGONALLY AWAY FROM THE FENCE ALONG A FAINT PATH THAT TAKES
YOU TO A GATE LEADING OUT ONTO OPEN MOORLAND. FOLLOW THE NARROW SHEEP TRACK
WHICH SOON DROPS GENTLY DOWN THE SLOPE. CROSS ANOTHER SMALL TRACK
AND CONTINUE DOWNWARDS. EVENTUALLY YOU DROP INTO A SMALL GULLY AND GO
THROUGH A GATEWAY INTO A FIELD ON THE RIGHT. CROSS THE FIELD, KEEPING THE
FENCE ON YOUR LEFT UNTIL YOU PICK UP A TRACK THAT DROPS DOWN INTO A LARGE
GULLY WITH A FORD AT THE BOTTOM. BEYOND THE FORD FOLLOW THE TRACK ACROSS A
BOGGY FIELD TO A JUNCTION AND TURN LEFT. A FEW YARDS FURTHER ON WHERE THE
TRACK SWINGS TO THE LEFT GO STRAIGHT ON ALONG A VAGUE GRASSY PATH. AFTER
GOING THROUGH A COUPLE OF GATES THE TRACK DISAPPEARS COMPLETELY BENEATH A
BRACKEN JUNGLE. FIGHT YOUR WAY STRAIGHT THROUGH FOR A COUPLE OF HUNDRED
YARDS UNTIL YOU MEET A GOOD CLEAR TRACK. (IF IN DOUBT BEAR SLIGHTLY
LEFT). TURN RIGHT (EFFECTIVELY STRAIGHT ON) ON THE TRACK AND FOLLOW IT
DOWN THE VALLEY. GO THROUGH A COUPLE OF GATES INTO A FIELD AND CONTINUE
STRAIGHT ON WITH THE HEDGE ON YOUR RIGHT. AT THE END OF THE FIELD TURN RIGHT
THROUGH A GATEWAY AND ALONG TO A CLEAR FARM TRACK. FOLLOW THIS TRACK,
BETWEEN HIGH HEDGES, DOWN THE VALLEY. AFTER ¾ MILE (1KM) YOU REACH TARMAC
AND CONTINUE ALONG THE ROAD TO A CROSSROADS.

GO STRAIGHT ACROSS THE CROSSROADS. AFTER A MILE (1·5KM) TURN RIGHT, THEN
¾ MILE (1KM) FURTHER ON TURN RIGHT AGAIN UP A STEEP NARROW ROAD. AFTER A
SHORT CLIMB THE ROAD LEVELS OFF AND BECOMES GRASSY AND OVERGROWN. FOLLOW
IT DOWN THROUGH A FORD AND CONTINUE STRAIGHT ON ALONG A SMOOTH CLEAR TRACK.
AFTER A COUPLE OF HUNDRED YARDS THIS TRACK BECOMES TARMAC, BUT A FEW
YARDS FURTHER ON IT SWINGS SHARPLY ROUND TO THE LEFT AND YOU CONTINUE
STRAIGHT ON UP A TRACK FOLLOWING THE HEDGE. AFTER GOING THROUGH A GATE
THIS BECOMES A SUPERB 2 MILE (3KM) TRACK ACROSS EMPTY MOORLAND WITH
EXCELLENT VIEWS.

EVENTUALLY THE TRACK DROPS DOWN THE FAR SIDE OF THE HILL. GO THROUGH

A GATE AND FOLLOW THE STEEP GRASSY TRACK DOWN THE SLOPE TO EVENTUALLY EMERGE, BEYOND A COTTAGE, ONTO TARMAC. FOLLOW THE ROAD DOWNHILL TO A T-JUNCTION. TURN RIGHT AND THEN RIGHT AGAIN AT ANOTHER T-JUNCTION ABOUT A MILE (1·5 KM) FURTHER ON. AFTER ANOTHER MILE (1·5 KM) TURN RIGHT UP THE SMALL ROAD TO GLASCWM. TURN RIGHT (YET AGAIN!) AT THE NEXT JUNCTION AND CONTINUE UP THE VALLEY TO THE TINY HAMLET OF GLASCWM. OPPOSITE THE LITTLE YOUTH HOSTEL TURN LEFT AND THEN AT A LEFT TURN GO STRAIGHT ON UP TO A GATE. GO THROUGH AND FOLLOW THE LITTLE ROAD UP THE SLOPE. AFTER A COUPLE OF HUNDRED YARDS GO STRAIGHT ON, FOLLOWING THE CLEAR TRACK. THIS TRACK CLIMBS STEADILY UP THE VALLEY, PASSING BETWEEN FIELDS AND THEN TAKING YOU UP ONTO OPEN MOORLAND. OVER THE TOP OF THE RISE THE TRACK BECOMES A FAST DESCENT DOWN THE FAR SIDE. DROP DOWN TO A GATE AND THEN FOLLOW THE SMOOTH TRACK WHICH EVENTUALLY BECOMES TARMAC LEADING STEEPLY DOWN INTO THE VALLEY.

WHEN YOU REACH A T-JUNCTION TURN LEFT AND ROLL ALONG THE MAIN ROAD FOR ¼ MILE (0·5 KM) TO HUNDRED HOUSE. (NO THERE AREN'T A HUNDRED HOUSES HERE. A HUNDRED WAS ORIGINALLY A SUBDIVISION OF A COUNTY. THE 'HUNDRED HOUSE' WAS PROBABLY THE COURT HOUSE FOR THE AREA.) OPPOSITE THE POST OFFICE (WITH PETROL PUMPS OUTSIDE!) TURN RIGHT AND FOLLOW THE ROAD TO FRANK'S BRIDGE. AFTER A MILE (1·5 KM) YOU RIDE THROUGH THE LITTLE HAMLET AND THEN A COUPLE OF HUNDRED YARDS FURTHER ON TURN LEFT TOWARDS THE SCHOOL. TURN RIGHT IN FRONT OF THE LITTLE SCHOOL BUILDING AND CONTINUE ALONG THE TARMAC TO A LEFT BEND. SWING OFF THE ROAD ON THE RIGHT TO A SMALL GATE AT THE START OF A DARK SUNKEN LANE, ITS A BIT ROUGH DOWN HERE - ESPECIALLY WHEN ITS WET- BUT JUST ABOUT RIDEABLE. AT THE END OF THE TRACK TURN LEFT INTO A FIELD CORNER THEN RIGHT ONTO A CLEAR TRACK THROUGH A SMALL OAK WOOD. AFTER A LITTLE WAY THE TRACK GOES THROUGH A FORD AND UP A SHORT CLIMB. AT THE TOP TURN LEFT ONTO A GRASSY TREE-LINED LANE. (GO ROUND THE LEFT HAND END OF THE BARBED WIRE FENCE.) THIS TRACK IS A BIT OF A CHALLENGE - WITH OVERHANGING BRANCHES TO LIMBO UNDER AND STICKS AND STONES LURKING BENEATH THE LONG GRASS. ITS ALL GOOD FUN THOUGH! AFTER ½ MILE (0·75 KM) AND VARIOUS GATES YOU GO THROUGH A GATE ON YOUR LEFT (BY A BRIDLEWAY SIGN) AND ONTO A SMALL ROAD. TURN RIGHT (EFFECTIVELY CARRYING ON IN THE DIRECTION OF THE TRACK) AND FOLLOW THE ROAD TO A JUNCTION. TURN RIGHT AND THEN RIGHT AGAIN AT THE NEXT JUNCTION. ZOOM ALONG THE MAIN ROAD FOR ¾ MILE (1 KM) THEN TURN LEFT UP A SMALL ROAD.

AFTER ½ MILE (0·75 KM) CONTINUE STRAIGHT UP A TRACK WHERE THE ROAD SWINGS AWAY TO THE RIGHT TOWARDS A FARM. WHEN YOU REACH A GATE GO THROUGH AND CONTINUE UP THE EDGE OF A COUPLE OF FIELDS. IN A THIRD FIELD CARRY ON UP A FAINT GRASSY TRACK AWAY FROM THE FENCE TO REACH ANOTHER GATE. GO THROUGH, FOLLOW THE FENCE ON YOUR RIGHT PAST A BARN, THROUGH ANOTHER GATE AND

ACROSS TO THE NEXT GATE WHERE YOU PICK UP AN OBVIOUS TRACK. FOLLOW
THIS ROUND THE HILLSIDE, THROUGH ANOTHER GATE AND ALONG TO ... YET
ANOTHER GATE. DON'T GO THROUGH THIS ONE – BUT TURN RIGHT UP A FAINT PATH
BESIDE THE FENCE. WHEN YOU REACH ANOTHER TRACK TURN LEFT AND GO
THROUGH THE GATE. ZOOM DOWN THE TRACK, ACROSS SOME OTHER TRACKS
AND KEEP GOING IN A STRAIGHT LINE ALONG A GRASSY PATH. WHEN YOU REACH
ANOTHER GATE GO THROUGH AND FOLLOW A FENCE ON YOUR LEFT. YOU SOON
FIND YOURSELF ON A GRASSY TRACK CUT INTO THE STEEP HILLSIDE. FOLLOW
THIS FOR 3/4 MILE (1KM) TO THE FINAL DESCENT BACK TO THE START.

THINGS TO SEE ─ WELSH HISTORY

IT'S DIFFICULT TO IGNORE HISTORY IN WALES. WHEREVER YOU GO YOU'LL FIND THE FINGERS OF THE PAST REACHING OUT INTO MODERN LIFE ─ WHETHER IN THE LANGUAGE OR CULTURE WITH THEIR CELTIC ORIGINS OR IN THE ANCIENT MOSS COVERED RUINS THAT LITTER THE LANDSCAPE.

THE FIRST TRACES OF PEOPLE IN WALES DATE FROM AN AMAZING 250,000 YEARS AGO. BUT THE PLACES THAT THESE EARLY CAVEMEN INHABITED WOULD HAVE BEEN COMPLETELY UNRECOGNISABLE TODAY. BRITAIN THEN WAS STILL CONNECTED TO MAINLAND EUROPE, AND THE HILLS AND MOUNTAINS THAT ARE SUCH A DISTINCTIVE PART OF THE WELSH LANDSCAPE HAD YET TO BE CARVED INTO THEIR MODERN SHAPES BY ICE AGE GLACIERS.

THE FIRST INHABITANTS OF MODERN WALES ARRIVED AROUND 10,000 YEARS AGO AS THE WEATHER WARMED UP AGAIN AFTER THE LAST ICE AGE. THESE STONE AGE PEOPLE LED A NOMADIC LIFE ─ LIVING IN CAVES OR TEMPORARY CAMPS AND REGULARLY MOVING ON IN SEARCH OF PLANTS AND ANIMALS FOR FOOD. GRADUALLY THEIR SETTLEMENTS BECAME PERMANENT AS THEY LEARNT TO GROW PLANTS AND KEEP ANIMALS. EARLY TOOLS WERE SIMPLY BITS OF STONE ─ USUALLY SHARPENED PIECES OF FLINT ─ BUT ABOUT 4000 YEARS AGO THERE WAS A MAJOR BREAK THROUGH WITH THE DISCOVERY OF METALS. BRONZE AGE CRAFTSMEN MADE METAL TOOLS AND WEAPONS ─ BUT THEY ALSO USED BRONZE, COPPER AND GOLD TO MAKE INTRICATE JEWELLERY.

AROUND 2500 YEARS AGO THE IRON AGE BEGAN, WITH THE ARRIVAL IN BRITAIN OF CELTIC CULTURE AND TECHNOLOGY FROM SOUTH-EAST EUROPE. PEOPLE BEGAN TO GROUP TOGETHER INTO WARLIKE TRIBES. WEAPONS BECAME MORE SOPHISTICATED AND HILLFORTS WERE BUILT FOR PROTECTION ON MANY HILLTOPS THROUGHOUT WALES AND THE MARCHES.

IMPRESSIVE THOUGH THE HILLFORTS WERE, THEY WERE NO MATCH FOR THE MIGHTY ROMAN ARMY WHICH INVADED BRITAIN IN AD 43. ALTHOUGH THE WELSH MOUNTAINS OFFERED SOME PROTECTION FOR THE LOCAL TRIBES IT WAS NOT LONG BEFORE THE WHOLE OF ENGLAND

AND WALES HAD BEEN CONQUERED. ROMAN ROADS, FORTS AND TOWNS SPREAD THROUGHOUT BRITAIN, AND WALES WAS VALUED FOR THE PRODUCE OF ITS FARMS AND MINES. ROMAN RULE FINALLY ENDED AT THE START OF THE FIFTH CENTURY WHEN THE ROMAN ARMY IN BRITAIN REBELLED AGAINST THE EMPEROR AND INVADED GAUL. BRITAIN WAS LEFT UNDEFENDED AND THE GRADUAL COLLAPSE OF THE EMPIRE MEANT THAT THE ROMANS NEVER RETURNED.

MEANWHILE THE EAST COAST OF BRITAIN HAD BECOME A FAVOURITE DESTINATION FOR GERMAN WARRIORS (ON PLUNDER AND PILLAGE PACKAGE TOURS!) NOW WITH BRITAIN LEFT DEFENCELESS THEY BEGAN TO ATTACK IN FORCE. SOON THE ANGLES AND SAXONS CONTROLLED ALL OF EASTERN BRITAIN AND THE BRITISH WERE PUSHED BACK INTO SCOTLAND, WALES AND THE FAR SOUTH-WEST. THE BORDER BETWEEN ENGLAND (ANGLELAND) AND THE BRITISH (IN WHAT CAME TO BE KNOWN AS WALES) WAS TO BE THE SUBJECT OF MANY CENTURIES OF CONFLICT. THE MOST IMPRESSIVE ATTEMPT TO FIX A PERMANENT BOUNDARY CAME IN THE LATE 8TH CENTURY WHEN KING OFFA BUILT A HUGE DYKE TO SEPARATE HIS LAND IN ENGLAND FROM THE WELSH. OFFA'S DYKE CONSISTED OF A DITCH AND AN EARTH BANK TOPPED WITH A WOODEN FENCE WHICH STRETCHED FOR 150 MILES (240 KM) BETWEEN THE SEVERN AND DEE ESTUARIES.

CUT OFF FROM THEIR COMPATRIOTS TO THE EAST, THE WELSH INCREASINGLY LOOKED WEST TO CONTACT WITH THE IRISH. ONE OF THE PRODUCTS OF THESE LINKS WERE THE WELSH SAINTS - IRISH CHRISTIAN MISSIONARIES WHO CROSSED THE SEA TO CONVERT THE PAGAN WELSH. MOST FAMOUS WAS SAINT DAVID WHO BECAME PATRON SAINT OF WALES. OTHERS WERE MORE OBSCURE - OR EVEN BIZARRE - SUCH AS SAINT MELANGELL THE PATRON SAINT OF HARES - OR SAINT DWYNWEN WHO BECAME THE PATRON SAINT OF LOVERS AFTER TURNING HER FIANCÉ INTO A BLOCK OF ICE!

DARK AGE WALES WAS SPLIT INTO SMALL TRIBAL KINGDOMS (GWYNEDD AND POWYS SURVIVE AS COUNTIES TODAY) WHICH SEEMED TO BE CONSTANTLY FEUDING WITH EACH OTHER. MEANWHILE ENGLAND WAS GRADUALLY COMING TOGETHER AS A SINGLE POWERFUL COUNTRY AND WAS AN EVER GROWING THREAT TO ITS WELSH NEIGHBOURS. IN 1066 THE DUKE OF NORMANDY, WILLIAM THE CONQUEROR, DEFEATED THE ENGLISH KING HAROLD AT THE BATTLE OF HASTINGS.

THE NEW KING WILLIAM REWARDED SOME OF THE POWERFUL NORMAN WARLORDS WHO HAD HELPED HIM WITH LAND IN THE MARCHES, AND THEY WERE ENCOURAGED TO EXPAND THEIR TERRITORY WESTWARDS INTO WALES.

THE NEXT TWO CENTURIES SAW A LONG SERIES OF BLOODY INVASIONS. BY THE MIDDLE OF THE TWELFTH CENTURY THE WELSH RULERS HAD BEEN FORCED TO STOP CALLING THEMSELVES KINGS AND WERE MERELY LORDS UNDER THE RULE OF THE KING OF ENGLAND. THE WELSH WERE HARDLY SUBMISSIVE THOUGH, AND FOR MANY YEARS ARMIES SWEPT TO AND FRO ACROSS THE BORDER IN A SERIES OF VIOLENT ATTACKS AND COUNTER-ATTACKS. WELSH RESISTANCE FINALLY REACHED A PEAK UNDER LLYWELYN AP GRUFFUDD (LLYWELYN THE LAST). BUILDING ON THE SUCCESS OF HIS GRANDFATHER (LLYWELYN THE GREAT - LORD OF GWYNEDD WHO HAD UNITED THE OTHER WELSH LORDS UNDER HIS CONTROL) HE REACHED THE PEAK OF HIS POWER IN 1267 WHEN HE FORCED THE WEAK ENGLISH KING HENRY III TO RECOGNISE HIM AS 'PRINCE OF WALES'. BUT WHEN HENRY III DIED HE WAS REPLACED BY THE FORMIDABLE EDWARD I. LLYWELYN SOON PUSHED HIS LUCK TOO FAR - PROVOKING EDWARD INTO LAUNCHING A DEVASTATING INVASION OF WALES. LLYWELYN WAS FINALLY KILLED IN A BATTLE NEAR BUILTH IN 1282 AND HIS SEVERED HEAD WAS DISPLAYED IN LONDON AS A SYMBOL OF EDWARD I's VICTORY. A STRING OF MASSIVE CASTLES WERE BUILT IN WALES BY EDWARD TO TOTALLY CRUSH ANY FURTHER ATTEMPTS AT WELSH INDEPENDENCE.

GRADUALLY THE INVADERS IMPOSED PEACE ON WALES. IN THE 1530's HENRY VIII PASSED THE ACTS OF UNION - UNITING WALES AND ENGLAND AND GIVING THE WELSH EQUAL RIGHTS INSTEAD OF TREATING THEM AS A CONQUERED NATION. WALES AND THE MARCHES WERE ADMINISTERED BY A COUNCIL BASED AT LUDLOW CASTLE. MEANWHILE MANY OTHER CASTLES HAD FALLEN INTO DISUSE. BUT WHEN ENGLAND ERUPTED INTO CIVIL WAR IN THE 1640's MUCH OF WALES SUPPORTED THE KING, AGAINST THE PARLIAMENTARIANS, AND THE OLD CASTLES WERE HASTILY PATCHED UP AND GARRISONED WITH TROOPS. WALES AND THE MARCHES WERE THE SCENE OF A NUMBER OF BLOODY BATTLES BEFORE THE ROYALISTS WERE FINALLY DEFEATED. ALTHOUGH MOST CASTLES STOOD UP WELL TO THE ATTACKS MANY WERE LATER WRECKED BY THE PARLIAMENTARIAN

SOLDIERS TO PREVENT THEM FROM EVER BEING USED AGAIN.

THE INDUSTRIAL REVOLUTION OF THE 18TH AND 19TH CENTURIES CHANGED THE FACE OF MUCH OF BRITAIN. MINING FOR COAL, IRON ORE AND OTHER MINERALS AND THE PRODUCTION OF IRON AND STEEL TRANSFORMED LARGE PARTS OF SOUTH WALES, SHROPSHIRE AND NORTH-EAST WALES. MEANWHILE SLATE QUARRYING WAS RIPPING HUGE HOLES OUT OF THE SIDES OF THE MOUNTAINS OF SNOWDONIA. IN MID-WALES, BY CONTRAST, INDUSTRY WAS MOSTLY ON A MUCH SMALLER SCALE. LEAD, COPPER, SILVER AND GOLD WERE FOUND IN SMALL POCKETS, BUT OTHER MATERIALS WERE MOSTLY ONLY MINED OR QUARRIED FOR LOCAL USE. THE ABUNDANT SUPPLY OF LOCAL WOOL WAS USED BY TEXTILE INDUSTRIES IN LLANIDLOES AND NEWTOWN. AN UNUSUAL FEATURE OF WELSH INDUSTRIES WAS THE USE OF NARROW GAUGE RAILWAYS FOR TRANSPORT. THESE WERE CHEAPER AND EASIER TO CONSTRUCT IN THE MOUNTAINOUS TERRAIN AND PROVIDED VITAL CONNECTIONS TO MANY REMOTE VILLAGES, AS WELL AS TO THE QUARRIES AND MINES.

WHILST INDUSTRY BROUGHT PROSPERITY FOR A FEW ENTREPRENEURS AND LAND OWNERS, THE MAJORITY OF WORKERS SUFFERED FROM APPALLING CONDITIONS AND POOR PAY. MANY LOOKED FOR COMFORT IN RELIGION, ESPECIALLY METHODISM, LEADING TO THE BUILDING OF CHAPELS IN MOST TOWNS AND VILLAGES. MEANWHILE, OTHERS WERE LOOKING FOR MORE RADICAL SOLUTIONS TO THEIR PROBLEMS. IN THE 1830's CHARTISTS BEGAN CAMPAIGNING FOR POLITICAL REFORMS. THEIR ACTIONS OFTEN RESULTED IN MAJOR DISTURBANCES - SUCH AS IN 1835 WHEN A GROUP RIOTED IN LLANIDLOES AND TOOK CONTROL OF THE TOWN FOR FOUR DAYS UNTIL THE ARMY ARRIVED. VIOLENT UNREST ALSO SPREAD AMONGST FARM WORKERS, LEADING TO THE BIZARRE REBECCA RIOTS OF THE LATE 1830's IN WHICH GANGS OF MEN DRESSED AS WOMEN ROAMED THE COUNTRYSIDE SMASHING TURNPIKE GATES.

TODAY MID-WALES AND THE MARCHES OFTEN SEEM LIKE QUIET AND SLEEPY PLACES. BUT AS YOU RIDE THE ROUTES IN THIS BOOK LOOK OUT FOR ANCIENT STONES, OVERGROWN RUINS AND OTHER RELICS OF THE PAST THAT HINT AT THE FASCINATING HISTORY OF THESE LANDS AND PEOPLE.

LLYN BRIANNE RESERVOIR HAS BEEN CREATED BY DAMMING THE STEEP SIDED VALLEY OF THE AFON TYWI. OUR DEMANDS FOR CLEAN FRESH WATER HAVE HAD A DRAMATIC IMPACT ON THE VALLEY - BUT IT STILL PROVIDES ENJOYABLE RIDING ON THE SMOOTH TRACKS AROUND THE LAKE AND THROUGH THE FOREST.

THE AFON DOETHIE HAS PERHAPS ONE OF THE PRETTIEST VALLEYS IN WALES. IT'S MORE THAN JUST A SCENIC GEM THOUGH - THE ROUTE DOWN THE VALLEY INCLUDES 4½ MILES (7 KM) OF TRULY BRILLIANT SINGLETRACK.

AFON DOETHIE

LLYN BRIANNE

START

AFON TYWI

AFON DINAS

N

1 KM

1 MILE

LLANWRTYD WELLS

RHANDIRMWYN

CILYCWM

A483

LLANDOVERY

LLYN BRIANNE & THE AFON DOETHIE

MAP: LANDRANGER 147   PATHFINDERS 990 + 1013
DISTANCE: 18½ MILES / 29.5 KM   OFFROAD: 13½ MILES / 21.5 KM
TIME: 3 - 4½ HOURS
HIGHEST POINT: 1450 FT / 440 M
TOTAL CLIMBING: 2000 FT / 610 M
START: LLYN BRIANNE DAM   793 485

START FROM THE CARPARK BESIDE THE DAM. CROSS THE BRIDGE
OVER THE OVERFLOW CHUTE AND RIDE ALONG THE TOP OF THE DAM.
THE LAKE STRETCHES AWAY TO YOUR RIGHT WHILST TO YOUR LEFT YOU
LOOK DOWN INTO THE VALLEY OF THE RIVER TYWI WITH ITS STEEP, ROCKY
SIDES AND THE DRAMATIC WATERSPOUT AT THE BOTTOM OF THE DAM.

AT THE END OF THE DAM SWING RIGHT ALONG THE LAKE SHORE ON A
SMOOTH WIDE TRACK. AFTER 1 MILE (1.5 KM) YOU ENTER A FOREST.
NAVIGATION THROUGH THE FOREST IS PRETTY EASY - JUST KEEP FOLLOWING
THE OBVIOUS MAIN TRACK. AFTER PASSING A CLEARING WITH A FARMHOUSE
ABOUT A MILE (1.5 KM) INTO THE FOREST, THE TRACK SWINGS LEFT
AND THEN, FURTHER ON, LEFT AGAIN TURNING UP A SIDE VALLEY
AWAY FROM THE LAKE. ABOUT ¾ MILE (1 KM) UP THIS VALLEY
THE TRACK SWINGS RIGHT, ACROSS A STREAM AND CLIMBS
GENTLY UP THE VALLEY SIDE, HEADING BACK DOWN THE VALLEY.
AFTER GAINING A LITTLE HEIGHT THE TRACK SWINGS LEFT AND
TAKES YOU TO A CLEAR FELLED AREA WHERE YOU COME TO A
T-JUNCTION. TURN LEFT, THEN AFTER ¾ MILE (1 KM) BEAR
RIGHT TO LEAVE THE FOREST.

FOLLOW THE TRACK ACROSS OPEN MOORLAND THEN GENTLY
DOWN INTO THE NEXT VALLEY ON A BRILLIANT SMOOTH, FAST
1 MILE (1.5 KM) DESCENT. THROUGH A GATE AND CONTINUE ALONG
THE TRACK FOR ANOTHER MILE TO SOAR Y MYNYDD - WHICH IS
CLAIMED TO BE THE MOST REMOTE CHAPEL IN WALES. TURN LEFT
UP THE STEEP ROCKY TRACK JUST PAST THE BUILDING. AFTER A
FEW HUNDRED YARDS OF LEG AND LUNG TORTURE THE TRACK
BECOMES A LITTLE EASIER AND LEADS UP ONTO THE BLEAK,
OPEN MOORLAND. THIS TRACK CAN GET VERY WET IN WINTER AND
THE DESCENT INTO THE VALLEY OF THE AFON DOETHIE IS ALSO
WET AND ROCKY. HALFWAY DOWN YOU GO THROUGH A GATE.
CONTINUE DOWNHILL FOR ANOTHER ¼ MILE (⅓ KM) THEN
LOOK FOR A TINY FAINT PATH ON YOUR LEFT BY A ZIG ZAG IN THE
TRACK. (THIS IS EASY TO MISS - ESPECIALLY IF YOU'RE RIDING FAST

AND CONCENTRATING ON THE ROCKY TRACK. LOOK OUT FOR A RICKETY LITTLE STILE ON THE RIGHT OPPOSITE THE START OF THE PATH.) TURN LEFT ONTO THE LITTLE PATH.

THIS IS THE START OF 4½ MILES (7KM) OF TOTALLY BRILLIANT SINGLETRACK. NAVIGATION IS SIMPLE - JUST KEEP FOLLOWING THE PATH DOWN THE VALLEY (ALTHOUGH BEWARE IN LATE SUMMER AND AUTUMN WHEN BRACKEN MAY OBSCURE THE PATH IN SOME PLACES). THERE ARE ROCKS, BUMPS, MUD, ROCKY STREAM CROSSINGS, TWISTY ROOTY SECTIONS THROUGH PATCHES OF TREES AND NARROW LEDGES ABOVE THE SWIRLING RIVER. THE SCENERY IS JUST AS BRILLIANT AS THE RIDING, WITH THE WATERS OF THE AFON DOETHIE TWISTING AND RUSHING BETWEEN THE STEEP VALLEY SIDES SCATTERED WITH ROCKY CRAGS, GNARLED OLD TREES AND THE RUINS OF ANCIENT FARMS. EACH BEND BRINGS ANOTHER SUPERB VIEW AND ANOTHER SET OF RIDING CHALLENGES. EVENTUALLY YOU PASS THROUGH A SMALL PATCH OF PINE TREES TO A GATE AND EMERGE INTO FIELDS. FOLLOW THE PATH ALONG TO A FARM TRACK AND BEAR LEFT ALONG IT TO A FARM, BEYOND WHICH YOU RETURN TO TARMAC.

THE ROUGH STUFF MAY BE OVER BUT THE SCENERY CERTAINLY ISN'T. IN FACT THE GENTLE CRUISE DOWN THE QUIET LANE GIVES YOU AN IDEAL OPPORTUNITY TO ADMIRE THE BEAUTY OF YOUR SURROUNDINGS. (IT'S WORTH MAKING REPEAT VISITS SO YOU CAN ENJOY THE DIFFERENT SEASONS OF THE ANCIENT OAK WOODLAND THAT CLOAKS THE VALLEY SIDES). CROSS THE RIVER ON A RICKETY BRIDGE AND CONTINUE UNTIL YOU EVENTUALLY CROSS ANOTHER BRIDGE AND COME TO A T-JUNCTION. TURN LEFT FOR THE STEADY 3 MILE (5KM) CLIMB BACK UP TO THE DAM.

ALONG THE ROAD YOU PASS DINAS - THE STEEP SIDED HILL ON THE LEFT. THIS HILL HAS A REPUTATION AS A SANCTUARY. A CAVE NEAR THE SUMMIT WAS ONCE THE HIDE-OUT OF TWM SIÔN CATTI - A KIND OF WELSH ROBIN HOOD. EVENTUALLY HE GAVE UP HIS LIFE OF ROBBING THE RICH TO MARRY ONE OF HIS VICTIMS - THE WIDOW OF THE SHERIFF OF CARMARTHEN. HE BECAME A RESPECTED MEMBER OF THE COMMUNITY AND WAS EVEN APPOINTED A JUSTICE OF THE PEACE. IN MORE RECENT TIMES DINAS WAS THE LAST NESTING SITE IN BRITAIN OF THE RED KITE, WHEN IT HAD ALMOST BECOME EXTINCT IN THIS COUNTRY. FORTUNATELY THE RED KITES ARE NOW RE-ESTABLISHING THEMSELVES THROUGHOUT WILD WALES AND THE HILL IS AN RSPB NATURE RESERVE TO PROTECT ALL THE BIRDS THAT LIVE THERE.

THE CISTERCIAN ABBEYS AT STRATA FLORIDA AND ABBEYCWMHIR WERE BU
IN THE 12TH CENTURY. THIS RIDE FOLLOWS THE ROUTE OF THE OLD MONK'S ROA
ACROSS THE EMPTY MOORLAND BETWEEN THE RUINS OF THE TWO ABBEYS. TH
RETURN TRIP TAKES YOU VIA RHAYADER AND THE CLAERWEN VALLEY WITH IT
HUGE RESERVOIR. THE ELAN LAKES ARE A CLEAR INDICATION OF HOW MUCH TH
AREA HAS CHANGED SINCE HENRY VIII CLOSED THE ABBEYS IN THE 16TH CENTU
BUT YOU CAN STILL APPRECIATE PLENTY OF THE PEACE AND NATURAL BEAUTY
THE MONKS CAME HERE TO FIND.

THIS ROUTE IS A SERIOUSLY TOUGH CHALLENGE. LONG AND ARDUOUS, IT
CROSSES BLEAK TERRAIN WITH BOGS, FORDS AND OTHER HAZARDS. THERE AR
3 WAYS IT CAN BE RIDDEN –
- STRATA FLORIDA TO ABBEYCWMHIR ONLY. THIS 30 MILE (49 KM) TRIP FOLLOWS
  THE MAIN PART OF THE MONK'S ROUTE - BUT YOU'LL NEED TO ARRANGE TO BE
  DROPPED OFF AT THE START AND PICKED UP AT THE FINISH.
- THE WHOLE ROUTE OVER 2 DAYS - WITH AN OVERNIGHT STOP HALFWAY.
- THE WHOLE ROUTE IN A DAY. PICK A LONG MID-SUMMER DAY, GET A GOOD
  EARLY START AND GO FOR IT!
WHICHEVER WAY YOU DO IT, IT'LL REQUIRE SOME PLANNING AND, UNLESS
YOU'RE ALREADY EXTREMELY FIT, SOME TRAINING.

START

LLYN
EGNANT

TO
PONTRHYD-
FENDIGAID

STRATA
FLORIDA
ABBEY

CLA

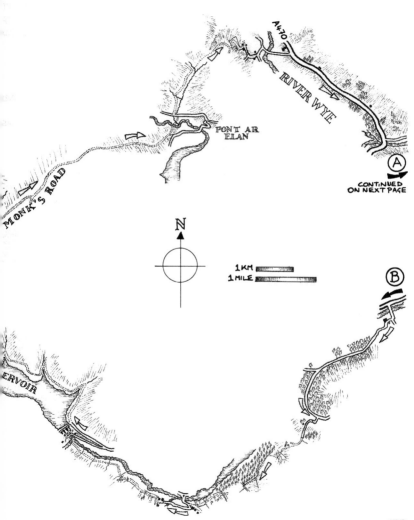

A470

RIVER WYE

PONT AR
ELAN

MONK'S ROAD

Ⓐ

CONTINUED
ON NEXT PAGE

N

1 KM
1 MILE

Ⓑ

ERVOIR

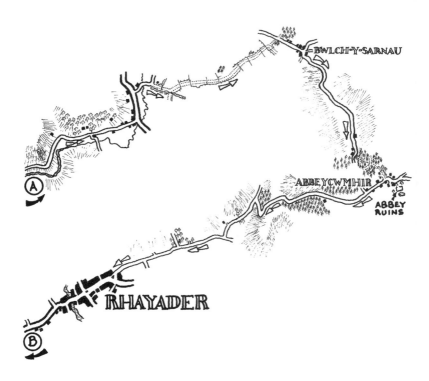

THE OLD MONK'S CHALLENGE ROUTE 25

MAP: LANDRANGER 147 OR PATHFINDERS 948, 949, 968, 969 (PLUS A VERY SMALL BIT OF 970).
DISTANCE: 62 MILES / 99 KM   OFFROAD: 33 MILES / 53 KM
TIME: 1-2 DAYS
HIGHEST POINT: 1780 FT / 542 M
TOTAL CLIMBING: 6900 FT / 2100 M
START: STRATA FLORIDA ABBEY   746 657

START OUTSIDE THE ABBEY RUINS AT STRATA FLORIDA. (PARKING IS A BIT LIMITED - THE CAR PARK IS FOR ABBEY VISITORS). WITH YOUR BACK TO THE ABBEY ENTRANCE BUILDING TURN RIGHT, THEN AFTER A FEW YARDS, RIGHT AGAIN UP A SMALL ROAD HEADING EAST UP THE VALLEY. 2 MILES (3 KM) OF EASY RIDING TAKES YOU UP TO THE END OF THE ROAD. JUST BEFORE A GATE TURN LEFT UP TO TYNCWM FARM. GO THROUGH THE FARM YARD AND THEN BEAR RIGHT, THROUGH A GATE AND UP

138

THE SLOPE TO A TRACK SWINGING LEFT UP THE VALLEY. THIS STEEP SIDED VALLEY HAS SOME BRILLIANT SCENERY – AND SOME SCARY DROPS DOWN TO THE ROCKY STREAM. FOLLOW THE TRACK UPWARDS UNTIL YOU EVENTUALLY REACH THE TINY ROAD BESIDE LLYN EGNANT. FOLLOW THE TARMAC PAST THE LAKE FOR A MILE (1·5KM) UNTIL YOU REACH A T-JUNCTION, WITH THE ROAD SWINGING AWAY TO THE LEFT AND A CLEAR GRAVEL TRACK TO THE RIGHT. TURN RIGHT ONTO THE TRACK.

AFTER A MILE (1·5KM) YOU SPLASH THROUGH A FORD. ABOUT 300 YARDS FURTHER ON BEAR LEFT WHERE THE TRACK FORKS (SIGNED TO RHYD HENGAE). AFTER THE FIRST FEW YARDS THIS TRACK BECOMES A BIT FAINT AND BOGGY. (BUT UNLESS ITS MISTY IT SHOULD BE EASY ENOUGH TO FOLLOW). CROSS THE HILLSIDE AND DROP DOWN TO THE RIVER CLAERWEN. THE FORD IS TOO ROCKY TO RIDE – SO CLIMB ACROSS USING THE STEPPING STONES. FOLLOW THE TRACK UP THE SLOPE BEYOND THE FORD. KEEP FOLLOWING THIS TRACK FOR THE NEXT 6 MILES (9·5 KM). IT CROSSES BLEAK AND FEATURELESS MOORLAND AND THERE ARE SOME DIFFICULT BOGGY AND RUTTED SECTIONS. EVENTUALLY YOU DESCEND TOWARDS THE ROAD NEAR THE END OF CRAIG GOCH RESERVOIR. HERE YOU CAN EITHER CONTINUE DOWN THE TRACK TO FORD THE RIVER ELAN. – OR YOU CAN TAKE THE SOFTIES OPTION – DROPPING DOWN ONTO THE ROAD AND CROSSING THE BRIDGE AT PONT AR ELAN. THE PENALTY FOR KEEPING YOUR FEET DRY IS AN EXTRA 170FT (50M) OF STEEP ROAD CLIMBING – BUT THERES OFTEN AN ICE CREAM VAN BY THE BRIDGE!

BEYOND THE FORD, FOLLOW THE TRACK TO THE ROAD. TURN LEFT OVER A SMALL BRIDGE AND THEN RIGHT ONTO A CLEAR TRACK. FOLLOW THIS TRACK UP A VALLEY FOR A MILE (1·5 KM) UNTIL IT TURNS SHARP LEFT UP A SIDE VALLEY. GO STRAIGHT ON, FOLLOWING FAINT SHEEP TRACKS UP TO THE HEAD OF THE VALLEY. SWING TO THE RIGHT ACROSS THE TOP OF THE PASS TO FIND A TRACK CARVED INTO THE SIDE OF A STEEP VALLEY DROPPING AWAY INFRONT OF YOU. FOLLOW THE TRACK DOWN THE HILL, WITH A SCARY LOOKING DROP ON YOUR LEFT. TURN LEFT AT A JUNCTION HALF WAY DOWN AND DROP DOWN TO A GATE. GO THROUGH AND CONTINUE DOWN THE FIELD IN A STEEP ZIG ZAG, TO A LANE DOWN TO A FARM. RIDE THROUGH THE FARMYARD AND TURN RIGHT DOWN THE FARM ROAD. AFTER ½ MILE (0·8 KM) TURN RIGHT AT A SORT OF T-JUNCTION (THE 3RD POSSIBLE RIGHT TURN) AND FOLLOW THE ROAD ACROSS THE RIVER WYE AND UP TO THE A470.

TURN RIGHT ON THE MAIN ROAD AND CRUISE DOWN THE SMOOTH TARMAC FOR 2½ MILES (4KM), THEN TURN LEFT ONTO A MINOR ROAD UP A SIDE VALLEY. FOLLOW THIS ROAD UP THE SCENIC VALLEY FOR 3 MILES (5KM). WHEN YOU REACH A T-JUNCTION BY A PUB TURN LEFT. TURN RIGHT AFTER ½ MILE (0·75KM), CROSS A COUPLE OF BRIDGES, THEN GO STRAIGHT ON ONTO A CLEAR TRACK WHERE THE ROAD BENDS ROUND TO THE LEFT. FOLLOW THIS TRACK, CLIMBING GENTLY AND PASSING THROUGH VARIOUS GATES FOR 2½ MILES (4KM). WHERE THE TRACK EVENTUALLY TURNS SHARP RIGHT, CONTINUE STRAIGHT ON ALONG A FIELD EDGE TO THE ROAD. TURN RIGHT ON THE ROAD AND RIDE ALONG TO THE LITTLE HAMLET OF BWLCH-Y-SARNAU. BEYOND THE HAMLET YOU CONTINUE DOWN THE QUIET LITTLE ROAD INTO A VALLEY. AFTER 2½ MILES (4KM)

Look out for a sign for the Coed Sarnau Forest Office on your right. Continue along the road, but after the next bend turn left down a dark sunken lane hidden between high hedges. Ride down through a ford then up the steep track through a forest. Go straight across when you meet other tracks and then at the top of the climb drop down the grassy track out of the forest, down a field edge and then down into Abbeycwmhir. Turn left on the road, opposite the pub. Ride through the village for 200 yards, then look for a wooden sign in a field on your right. Go through the gate and walk down to the abbey ruins. (Don't ride your bike down the field or around the abbey ruins).

There's not much left of the old abbey at Abbeycwmhir. It was partly destroyed by Owain Glyndŵr in 1402 and by the time it came to be closed by Henry VIII in the 1530's there were only 3 monks living here. During the Civil War it was a Royalist stronghold and was attacked by the Round Heads. Abandoned since then there's now no more than a few stunted walls where this once great building stood.

To return to Strata Florida head back through the village along the road. Continue straight on along the valley and then up a long road climb. The descent down the far side is steep and fast (watch out for sharp bends). At a T-junction at the bottom turn left. Then at the next T-junction turn right and follow the road for 2¼ miles (3.5km) to Rhayader. When you reach the main road turn right and ride into town. (There's plenty of shops, cafés and pubs here to tempt weary travellers). Go straight on past the clock tower, along the road towards the Elan Valley. About a mile (1.5km) from Rhayader turn left and cross a bridge over the Afon Elan. Swing round to the right at the next junction and follow the little road up the valley. Take the left fork after 1½ miles (2.5km), then after another mile (1.5km) turn right down an even smaller road. This takes you (via a gate) to a steep climb. At the top go through a gate and straight on up a track. When the track begins to descend towards a ruined farmhouse by a clump of trees, bear left onto a grassy path. Follow this track down to the left of the house, through some fords and round to a forest. Swing to the left up the forest edge then down a grassy descent to a ford. Go through the gate beyond, and follow a very faint grassy path across the field until you pick up a clear track at the farside. Follow the track through a ford, then down past Dolymynach Reservoir to a farm. Pass the farm and when you reach tarmac turn left. The little road swings round in a sharp zig zag before taking you up the valley to another farm. Ride into the farmyard, past a couple of barns, then turn right. Follow the obvious track up the valley for the next 2 miles (3km). The route is pretty easy to follow all the way but there are some rough, rocky and boggy sections – a real challenge for tired legs. Eventually you cross a wide ford below the Claerwen Dam. Cross a little field then

TURN RIGHT ON THE ROAD AND CROSS THE BRIDGE OVER THE RIVER CLAERWEN. FOLLOW THE ROAD BACK DOWN THE VALLEY FOR ½ MILE (0.8 KM) THEN SWING ROUND TO THE LEFT AND CLIMB UP TO THE TOP OF THE DAM.

WHERE THE ROAD TURNS LEFT ACROSS THE TOP OF THE DAM GO STRAIGHT ON ALONG THE CLEAR WIDE TRACK AROUND THE SIDE OF THE LAKE. THE NEXT 6½ MILES (10.5 KM) FOLLOW THE LAKESIDE TRACK (IGNORE ANY TRACKS LEADING OFF AWAY FROM THE RESERVOIR). EVENTUALLY, AFTER PASSING THE END OF THE LAKE, FORK LEFT DOWN TO A BRIDGE. CONTINUE ALONG THE TRACK (BEWARE - THERE ARE SOME MONSTER PUDDLES!). AFTER ABOUT A MILE (1.5 KM) YOU FIND YOURSELF BACK ON A FAMILIAR TRACK. FOLLOW IT BACK THE SAME WAY YOU CAME AT THE START OF THE RIDE. - BACK UNTIL YOU REACH TARMAC, LEFT DOWN PAST THE LAKE THEN STRAIGHT ON DOWN THE TRACK INTO THE VALLEY AND BACK DOWN THE ROAD TO STRATA FLORIDA.

▼ Strata Florida
Abbey

OTHER ROUTES

THE ROUTES IN THIS BOOK ARE A SELECTION OF SOME OF THE BEST MOUNTAIN BIKE RIDES IN MID-WALES AND THE MARCHES. BUT THERE ARE THOUSANDS OF MILES OF OTHER ROUTES, ALONG BRIDLEWAYS AND OTHER RIGHTS OF WAY, WAITING TO BE EXPLORED. THERE ARE ALSO SOME BRILLIANT SPECIALLY CREATED MOUNTAIN BIKE TRAILS.

COED Y BRENIN.

7 MILES (11KM) NORTH OF DOLGELLAU ON THE A470 LANDRANGER MAP 124, 716 278. FOREST ENTERPRISE HAVE REALLY PIONEERED THE PROVISION OF QUALITY MOUNTAIN BIKE TRAILS AND COED Y BRENIN IS ONE OF THEIR BEST. THERE ARE 3 MAIN ROUTES TO CHOOSE FROM RANGING FROM UNDER 7 MILES TO OVER 20, PLUS THE (HIGHLY RECOMMENDED) 7 MILE (11KM) RED BULL ROUTE - LAID OUT A BIT LIKE A RACE COURSE WITH PLENTY OF CHALLENGING SECTIONS FOR SKILLED RIDERS LOOKING FOR SOME FUN. THE SCENERY'S PRETTY GOOD TOO - WITH VIEWS OF THE SURROUNDING MOUNTAINS AND PICTURESQUE TRAILS BESIDE ROCKY RIVERS AND THROUGH PATCHES OF OLD OAK WOODLAND. FACILITIES INCLUDE PAY AND DISPLAY CAR PARK, TOILETS, PICNIC AREA AND (EASTER TO OCTOBER) VISITOR CENTRE, CAFÉ AND BIKE HIRE. RING 01766 87569 FOR MORE DETAILS AND TO BOOK BIKES.

HAFREN FOREST.

WEST OF CLYWEDOG RESERVOIR. LANDRANGER MAP 136, 857 869. MORE FOREST ENTERPRISE WAY-MARKED TRAILS. THE TWO ROUTES ARE FAIRLY SHORT AND EASY AND CLASSIFIED AS FAMILY TRAILS - SUITABLE FOR BEGINNERS OR AS SHELTERED RIDES IN WINTER. HAFREN IS THE WELSH NAME FOR THE RIVER SEVERN AND ONE OF THE ROUTES TAKES YOU UP NEAR THE RIVER'S SOURCE ON THE SLOPES OF PLYNLIMON. PAY + DISPLAY CAR PARK, PICNIC SITE AND TOILETS.

HOPTON MOUNTAIN BIKE TRAIL.

8 MILES (13KM) SOUTH-WEST OF CRAVEN ARMS. LANDRANGER MAP 137. AT HOPTON FOREST ENTERPRISE HAVE TRIED SOMETHING A BIT DIFFERENT. INSTEAD OF THE USUAL SET ROUTES THEY'VE CREATED A HUGE NETWORK OF INTERLINKING TRACKS THROUGH 860 ACRES OF FOREST. TO FIND YOUR WAY AROUND YOU'LL NEED TO BUY A COPY OF THE SPECIAL WATERPROOF TRAIL MAP BEFORE YOU GO (THE TRACKS AREN'T ALL SHOWN ON O.S. MAPS). THEN JUST MAKE UP YOUR ROUTE AS YOU GO. EACH JUNCTION HAS A NUMBERED MARKER POST - CHECK YOUR LOCATION ON THE MAP AND DECIDE WHAT TO TRY NEXT. SCARY DOWNHILLS, CHALLENGING CLIMBS, GNARLY SINGLETRACK AND GENTLE FOREST ROADS - THERE'S PLENTY OF EVERYTHING AND YOU'LL PROBABLY RUN OUT OF ENERGY LONG BEFORE YOU RUN OUT OF ROUTES TO TRY. BRILLIANT. MAPS ARE AVAILABLE FOR £1.25 (INC P+P) FROM: FOREST ENTERPRISE, MARCHES DISTRICT, WHITCLIFFE, LUDLOW, SY82HD. OR RING 01584 874542 FOR DETAILS.

FOREST ENTERPRISE ALLOW BIKES IN A NUMBER OF OTHER FORESTS - BUT CHECK BEFORE YOU RIDE - NOT ALL FORESTS ARE OWNED BY F.E. AND IN THOSE THAT ARE ACCESS MAY BE RESTRICTED BECAUSE OF FORESTRY OPERATIONS OR SENSITIVE WILDLIFE.

LLWYBR MAWDDACH TRAIL. BARMOUTH TO DOLGELLAU.

LANDRANGER MAP 124, 630 139 TO 715 183. THIS WALKING AND CYCLING TRAIL FOLLOWS THE SCENIC ROUTE OF THE OLD RAILWAY FOR 7 MILES (11·5 KM) UP THE ESTUARY FROM BARMOUTH BRIDGE TO DOLGELLAU. BEING FLAT ALL THE WAY IT MAKES AN EASY RIDE, BUT YOU CAN ALSO USE IT AS A LINK TO REACH TOUGHER TRACKS UP INTO THE HILLS ON EITHER SIDE OF THE ESTUARY. FOR REAL CHALLENGE SEEKERS ITS ALSO PART OF THE 288 MILE (460 KM) LÔN LAS CYMRU ROUTE FROM HOLYHEAD TO CARDIFF. CONTACT SUSTRANS, 35 KING ST, BRISTOL, BS1 4DZ, TEL: 0117 929 0888 FOR DETAILS.

NANT MAWR QUARRY. 4 MILES (6KM) SOUTH WEST OF OSWESTRY.

THIS DERELICT LIMESTONE QUARRY AND SURROUNDING LAND HAS BEEN TRANSFORMED INTO A CHALLENGING MOUNTAIN BIKE TRAIL. THE LAND IS ALL PRIVATELY OWNED AND ACCESS IS LIMITED TO MEMBERS ONLY. FOR MEMBERSHIP DETAILS CONTACT: NANTMAWR QUARRY LIMITED, NANTMAWR, OSWESTRY, SHROPSHIRE, SY10 9HL. TEL: 01691 659358.

JACK MYTTON WAY. BILLINGSLEY TO LLANFAIR WATERDINE.

LANDRANGER MAPS 137 + 138, 713 833 TO 245 759. THIS 70 MILE (120KM) BRIDLEROUTE IS NAMED AFTER A HISTORICAL LOCAL ECCENTRIC. THE ROUTE INCLUDES A FEW ECCENTRICITIES ITSELF – SUCH AS THE FACT THAT IT STARTS AND FINISHES IN OBSCURE PLACES IN THE MIDDLE OF NOWHERE. BUT TRAVELLING JUST FOR THE HELL OF IT, WITH NO REAL DESTINATION IS ONE OF THE BEST WAYS TO SEE THE MARCHES AND THIS ROUTE TAKES YOU THROUGH THE SUPERB SCENERY OF SOUTH SHROPSHIRE – ALONG WENLOCK EDGE, OVER THE LONG MYND, PAST OFFA'S DYKE AND DOWN INTO THE TEME VALLEY AND THE WELSH BORDER. FOR MORE INFORMATION CONTACT: SHROPSHIRE COUNTY COUNCIL LEISURE SERVICES DEPARTMENT, CHURCHILL BUILDING, RADBROOK ROAD, SHREWSBURY, SY3 9BJ.

RACES AND COMPETITIONS. IF COMPETITION GETS YOUR

ADRENALIN FLOWING YOU'LL FIND THERE ARE PLENTY OF RACES HELD REGULARLY THROUGHOUT THE REGION. THE HILLY TERRAIN PRODUCES EXCELLENT COURSES FOR BOTH CROSS COUNTRY AND DOWNHILL RACING AND A WIDE RANGE OF VENUES CATER FOR EVERYTHING FROM SMALL LOCAL EVENTS TO NATIONAL CHAMPIONSHIPS AND FAMOUS ODDITIES SUCH AS THE MAN VS HORSE VS BIKE. (REMEMBER – MOST RACES ARE HELD ON PRIVATE LAND AND THE COURSES ARE ONLY OPEN ON RACE WEEKENDS – DON'T TRY TO RIDE THEM AT OTHER TIMES.)

THERE ARE ALSO A WIDE RANGE OF OTHER COMPETITIONS AND EVENTS – FROM TRAILQUESTS (MOUNTAIN BIKE ORIENTEERING) TO BIKE AND BEER WEEKENDS! CHECK OUT THE EVENTS SECTIONS OF MOUNTAIN BIKE MAGAZINES FOR DETAILS OF WHAT'S ON.